MOVE OVER MR. HOLLAND

INSIGHTS, HUMOR, AND PHILOSOPHY ON MUSIC AND LIFE

TREY REELY

FOREWORD BY TIM LAUTZENHEISER

ILLUSTRATED BY VIRGINIA GIST

Grateful acknowledgment is made to
The Instrumentalist Company, Northfield, Illinois, for permission
to reprint Trey Reely's articles: "How to Succeed in Band" (April, 1990); "Inspired
Instrument Maintenance" (December, 1991); "Learning from Contest Comments
(August, 1993); "When I Was A Kid..." (previously titled "Remembering the Good
Old Days") (November, 1995); "Memories of a Lifetime" (August, 1997), "Articles
That Inspire" (September, 1997), "How to Lose Weight and Make Money"
(previously titled "Battle Hymn of the Bulge") (October, 1997); "Move Over Mr.
Holland" (June, 1997); "The Good News and the Bad News" (previously titled
"2001-A Space Odyssey") (December, 1997); "Bobby Jax" (previously titled "In Spite
of Me") (April, 1998); "Signs of the Times" (previously titled "Bandroom
Hazards") (May, 1998); "Gaining Perspective" (June, 1998), "Behind the
Times and Losing Ground (August, 1998), "Speech 101" (previously titled
"Tales That Terrify") (October, 1998), and "Just Chill," (February, 1999).
Subscribe to The Instrumentalist for 1 year, 12 issues for $24 (U.S. Delivery)
(200 Northfield Road, Northfield, Illinois - 847-446-8550)
Funky Winkerbean® cartoons reprinted with special permission of
North America Syndicate.

Author photo (see back cover) by John Kennett of Child Art Studio.
Cover design, illustrations, and pre-press work by
SculptNET Website Development – www.sculptnet.com
Audra Howerton, Creative Director
Virginia Gist, Designer and Illustrator.

ISBN 0-9673756-0-6
Library of Congress Catalog Card Number: 99-93450

Music • Humor • Education • Essays • Conducting • Band

"A delightful book with bits of wisdom encased in good humor."
—*Francis McBeth, Composer*

"*Move Over Mr. Holland* offers a quick laugh and lingering insight."
—*Tom O'Neal, Arkansas State University Director of Bands*

"[*Move Over Mr. Holland*] identifies a multitude of experiences, challenges, and problems and solutions which we all have been through, captures the essence of being a band director, and highlights a traditional and familiar daily routine . . . Several of the chapters were of particular interest to me, but I especially found 'Marching Through Wal-Mart' rich in ideas to involve students in constructive social activity. It seems that schools today are reluctant to take an active role in teaching discipline, hence the band director needs all of the tools he can find to keep the band student interested and productive."
—*Eldon Janzen, Author, The Band Director's Survival Guide*

". . . this homespun book gave me the opportunity to laugh, cry, and nod in agreement with the various thoughts and down-to-earth descriptions of a real-life Mr. Holland."
—*Tim Lautzenheiser, Motivational Speaker*

"Without a doubt, this book of band directing vignettes captures the essence of the humor and humanity found in our profession. 'When I Was A Kid . . . ' brought back many nostalgic memories and reflections. I couldn't stop laughing after reading 'Excuses, Excuses,' and 'Gaining Perspective' was an important chapter for teaching character and responsibility."

—*John W. Knight, Oberlin Conservatory of Music*

Contents

Dedication

The English poet John Donne rightly proposed that "no man is an island." It could likewise be suggested that "no musician is a soloist." Although musicians may appear to perform alone, there are many individuals past and present performing with them, their influences melded together into one entity. Our lives are bits and pieces of others who have added notes to our own personal, life-long composition—some dissonant, some consonant, but all necessary. I need look no further than my own father for the great consonances of my life.

I remember the day I decided to play trumpet. I was in fifth grade and a representative from the local music store came to our homeroom class to show us instruments. I was amazed that he could play every instrument he picked up, and I was most impressed with the trumpet. No other instrument stood a chance at gaining my attention once he played reveille on that shiny, gold-lacquered instrument. I couldn't explain it, but I was hooked.

My dad was particularly pleased with my choice because he played the cornet all the way through college, earning a degree in music from Florida State University before becoming a pilot in the Air Force. I know he was also pleased with the economical advantages since he still had the trusty silver Olds cornet that he used during his playing days.

I would have preferred a new instrument, but my parents assured me I would get a new trumpet if I continued my studies. My mom, a veteran of psychedelic ceramic and craft classes commonly held in the sixties, tried to help ease the burden of carrying an old, decrepit case by covering it with red, white, and blue contact paper so it would appear more socially acceptable. Being a typical, self-conscious adolescent, I was ashamed of the case once I got to school. I looked like I got lost on the way to Woodstock. To avoid the inevitable teasing, I put it in my cubbyhole as soon as possible each day.

Dad gave me a few lessons during my first year, but I was not as receptive as I should have been to his musical teaching. I have since discovered that is not unusual for children of musicians, but I regret it just the same.

Fortunately, this didn't discourage him from being a strong source of support. In eighth grade I was given a new Bach trumpet, and Dad secured a private instructor for me at a local university. When I became discouraged and felt too busy to take lessons, he didn't force me to continue but worked out a compromise whereby I could have a lesson once every two weeks. His strategy worked—instead of souring me on lessons, it kept me going until I was mature enough to realize I needed them every week.

> **He kept me focused on my strengths and their potential contribution to my success as a teacher, never letting my feelings of inadequacy overcome good sense.**

Later that year, Dad took me to a Maynard Ferguson concert. On the day of the concert, all the trumpet players in my section were talking about how high Ferguson could play. Since our music theory was rather weak, rumors of just how high he could play defied the laws of physics, acoustics and many other sciences. Nevertheless, Ferguson's performance was the most exciting thing I had ever heard or imagined.

As I matured I came to value my dad's advice. Through the ups and downs that are inevitable during high school and college, he helped me to keep things in perspective. During my college years there were times when I considered changing my major to something other than music. I spent too much time comparing myself unfavorably to others more gifted, individuals whose talents seemed to make their successes so effortless, while my own successes seemed to be accomplished only through hard-nosed determination.

An avid runner, Dad would take me on his daily jaunts through the neighborhood, and we would discuss many of my frustrations. As the miles passed he would listen patiently to my problems and then help break them down rationally, going over all the pros and cons of possible alternatives. He kept me focused on my strengths and their potential contribution to my success as a teacher, never letting my feelings of inadequacy overcome good sense.

In addition to Dad's support, I felt an irresistible pull—toward the trumpet specifically and a music career in general—that I just could not explain. I enjoyed many interests outside the musical realm that I could have pursued, but none seemed able to fulfill the deep-seated desires of my heart. Why was this?

Just a couple of years ago, I found a small clue—a photograph of my dad and me when I was thirteen months old. Sitting on his lap, I was apparently having my first cornet lesson, although I was probably more  interested in how to get the thing in my mouth. Nevertheless, my dad had piqued my interest much earlier than I had realized.

Educators say that many aspects of human personality are in place by the time a child reaches the age of four. I couldn't help thinking that, intentionally or not, Dad had planted little musical seeds in my mind. Did I have the irresistible love for the trumpet and music because of these experiences too early for conscious memory? I'll never know for sure, but of one thing I have little doubt—without my dad's constant encouragement, I wouldn't have the career in music I have now. Even the publication of this book would not have been possible without his undying support and advice. It is to my dad that I dedicate this book. Thanks, Dad.

Acknowledgements

I would be remiss if I did not mention others who made this book possible.

First, my mom. Long before the days of word processing, she typed my high school and college papers, using her considerable skill to save me much frustration. She was a great editor then and continues to help me today. In fact, she helped edit this manuscript. If it wasn't for the fact that I can now use a word processor, she might have typed the manuscript for this book!

My wife Ronda and children Ashton, Ryan, and Kelsey who have been quite tolerant of my "piddling around." I think they can see that at least some of the piddling turned into a book!

Bonnie Hamilton and Doris Hagen, two of my colleagues at Paragould High School, for their help in editing the original manuscript despite the pressure of having to grade a zillion research papers as well.

Virginia Gist, designer and illustrator for SculptNET Website Development, for her great work on the cover design and illustrations.

Ellen Meadows, journalist extraordinaire, and Adam Brawner—student, pianist, and tuba player—for graciously proofreading the final manuscript at a moment's notice just before the print deadline.

Cliff Ganus, my choral director at Harding University, for publishing my first article in 1989.

The band students and parents at Paragould Junior and Senior High School, the source and inspiration for many of my stories.

Assistant band director Terry Hogard whom I have had the honor to teach with for almost a decade.

Finally, Audra Howerton, creative director at SculptNET Website Development, for getting the book camera ready for the printer and being such an enthusiastic and conscientious supporter of this project.

Preface

In *Music, the Brain, and Ecstasy* Robert Jourdain states that "no human undertaking is so formidable as playing a musical instrument. Athletes and dancers may drive their bodies to greater exertions; scholars may juggle more elaborate conceptual hierarchies; painters and writers may project greater imagination and personality. But it is musicians who must draw together every aspect of mind and body, melding athleticism with intellect, memory, creativity, and emotion, all in gracious concert."

Statements such as this both inspire and depress me. I am inspired by the fact that what I do is challenging, but it is that very challenge that can be overwhelming. Can we really get our students to draw together every aspect of mind and body in the pursuit of musical excellence? Baseball players are great if they can bat over .300. Quarterbacks are praised if they complete sixty percent of their passes. And yet we must drive our students much further than that. How many musicians would be considered successful if they performed only thirty percent of the rhythms and sixty percent of the notes correctly?

Short attention spans cultivated in a culture bent towards instant gratification make the pursuit of musical excellence even more difficult. Disintegrating parental support, poverty, pursuit of the almighty dollar, and a host of other teenage concerns all vie with us for the hearts and minds of today's youth. It's terrifying to think that our livelihoods depend on how successfully we work with walking hormones growing up in such a social milieu.

I earnestly believe there is nothing in life that carries real meaning and value that does not require great effort. I stress to students that the commitment they make to musical excellence is something that they should apply to everything in life, both present and future. Within life's challenges rest the greatest of rewards. And what are the rewards for our musical pursuits?

Money? Unfortunately, our society has shown where its priorities are by how it spends its money. In his book *Piano Pieces*, pianist and author Russell Sherman writes about the time a friend commented to his teacher that the garbage truck driver they were watching out the window probably made more money than he did. "Perhaps," replied his teacher, "but somehow I'd rather play the piano."

How about trophies, plaques, or the "perfect" performance? Obviously, it is great to be recognized and rewarded for hard work and excellence, but these things are a meager diet without a sustained love for music itself and the process of imparting it to our students. If we're not careful, too much focus is placed on the destination rather than how we got there.

I sincerely believe that our reward is the incredible journey we are able to undertake. How many people get the opportunity to travel the road that we do? Like others, we have a life of ups and downs and inevitable detours, but what separates us from many is the fact that our journey is accompanied by music. Not music skillfully developed to reap profits, but music crafted with great toil and care by teachers and their students. Even more exciting is the fact that this is one journey that need not be completed. We need never arrive.

We should boldly embrace the journey of challenges that music presents and encourage students to do likewise. Once embraced, the challenges can be met in a way that results in a knowing sense of pride unshakable by the ignorant criticisms of peers and an oft-misguided public. For example, baseball slugger

Mark McGuire, baffled by his own unbelievable success at breaking Roger Maris' homerun record, said, "I am in awe of myself." Our students should be in awe of themselves for their ability to draw mind and body together to accomplish musical wonders.

It is my hope that this book helps you face the challenges of your incredible journey with music. This book is rather eclectic—the chapters range from serious to practical to humorous. If what I have written serves you in any way as a source of practical advice, reflection, encouragement, or comic relief, it will have been well worth the effort.

Foreword

Move Over Mr. Holland: Insights, Humor, and Philosophy on Music and Life is an incredibly refreshing perspective of what we encounter as band directors throughout our professional and personal lives. Reading this homespun book gave me the opportunity to laugh, cry, and nod in agreement with the various thoughts and down-to-earth descriptions of a real-life Mr. Holland. With his tongue in his cheek but his mind centered on reality, Trey leads us through chapter after chapter of honesty, laced with just enough exaggeration to tickle the funny bone.

Let's face it—band directors share many inside jokes. Haven't we all been in social settings with an array of different professionals, waiting for our chance to enter the conversation with one of our infamous band jokes or music anecdotes but when the moment arrives we share the best band joke we know—much like a major symphonic performance—only to have the punch line receive nothing more than an obligatory chuckle and a cold stare from our spouse? (I'll bet none of those people marched a six-mile parade carrying a bass drum!)

Perhaps what I enjoyed most about Trey's musings came at the very end of the book. In the final chapter "Memories of a Lifetime" he brings the reader full-circle and hits him right between the eyes with a dose of truth that had me reaching for tissues, many tissues. The final sentence says it all: "Our task, however daunting, is to remember that each student is an individual, making memories that will last a lifetime."

Many thanks are extended to Trey Reely— author, band director, teacher, and friend. Thank you for sharing your insights and special feelings concerning the world's greatest profession—band directing. Thanks for pushing us to the edge and allowing us to look at ourselves in a healthy light. Thank you for offering a bold reminder of why we do what we do.

You are going to love this book. It's time to "strike up the band." Read and enjoy.

—Tim Lautzenheiser

Homecomings
and Goings

Homecoming. Just the word itself strikes fear into a band director's heart. A hectic week of homecoming activities makes extended concentration difficult for students. Thoughts of what to wear, how to fix their hair, and who to ask to the homecoming dance often replace the musical thoughts directors wish were there in greater abundance. Many are busy building floats for the homecoming parade, painting backdrops for the queen's court, and sewing costumes for skits to be performed at the homecoming assembly.

Add the extra responsibilities that the band has during homecoming week, and the typical band student's problems are compounded even further. Setting a new field formation for the homecoming queen and her court takes precious rehearsal time as does practicing the accompanying heart-wrenching movie theme. (We considered playing "Beauty and the Beast" one year but thought better of it since the paternal escorts might be offended.) On the night before homecoming we perform at the school's traditional bonfire where, if we're lucky enough to have the wood actually catch on fire, we singe our eyebrows to the sounds of "Louie Louie" and other cheerleader favorites.

The director's stress level is particularly elevated when there is an important marching contest the day after homecoming. I made this mistake *once* and that year my band set the world record for most people sleepwalking at the same time. We should have done a theme show featuring lullabies and marched in our PJ's.

"Mr. Reely, your face looks funny!"

My memories of homecomings run together, but there is one I will remember more than any other since it has made all my other homecomings seem uneventful by comparison. That particular year, homecoming week was actually rather typical until the final day. A student approached me just before my first period rehearsal began and, with a casual bluntness only a student can use, said, "Mr. Reely, your face looks funny."

I wasn't sure what to make of this, but I did manage to respond, "I hate to disappoint you, but people have told me that my whole life."

Attempting to clarify, she said, "No, I mean funnier than usual . . . I mean . . . well, never mind."

After class I went to the teachers' lounge to see what was happening. I looked in the mirror, and I could see that my face was drawn down a little on the left. When I smiled, only the right side would work. I thought immediately that I probably had Bell's palsy. I wouldn't have suspected this except for the fact that I had a friend in college who had it. As I stared at my disfigured face, I wondered if I was looking at only the beginning of what might turn me into the Elephant Man by seventh period.

I also felt an odd sense of relief, because my now-obvious condition explained what I had experienced the evening before. I was giving a flute lesson to a new student, aware that she had no idea how effective a teacher I was, and each time I demonstrated a musical concept, the most awful sound would result. I would say, "It sounds like this" and then go on to produce a tone resembling air rushing through a sewer pipe. I even tried another flute and sounded just as bad. Apparently my mouth was already off-kilter. The weakness of the muscles on the affected side caused my face to be pulled to the normal side by the unopposed muscles. In other words my face was playing tug-of-war with itself and my left side was losing.

At lunch I made the mistake of mentioning my travails to my fellow teachers who were more than willing to offer up every worst case scenario for Bell's palsy one might imagine. "Yeah, I had an Uncle George who had that for nearly thirteen years" and "My Aunt Margaret's face got so distorted half of her face looked like a prune" were a couple of the milder sources of encouragement. By the end of my meal I was longing for a recovery group.

I also had fun hearing people's beliefs regarding the cause of my malady. Many of my students believed it was stress brought on by a particular phone call I had received that day. For weeks afterward, I would get funny looks from students when they saw me on the phone. They would look at me with raised eyebrows and shake their fingers. My doctor was rather clueless as to the exact origin of my condition as well, but he felt that my case was rather mild and should go away with medicine, facial exercises, and time. As I left the doctor's office, I figured that if I didn't smile it would be hard to notice that something was wrong. If I *did* smile I looked eerily like Elvis

> **. . . as soon as they saw I was really okay . . . the jokes started pouring in.**

Presley. If I could manage not to smile for a month, maybe no one would notice. I didn't smile my whole first year of teaching, so I knew it could be done.

My students were rather sympathetic at first, but as soon as they saw I was really okay and not suffering from anything fatal, the jokes started pouring in. They dubbed my condition "Bellsheimers," a cross I suppose between Alzheimer's and Bell's palsy. Despite my resolution, I couldn't help smiling at times and this spawned an endless train of Elvis jokes. I can't count how many times I was offered a jelly donut. Fortunately, the effects of Bell's palsy did not worsen and I recovered over the ensuing two weeks without suffering lasting effects.

I now enjoy homecomings a little more. After that difficult homecoming, the others have been easy by comparison. The way I look at it, if I don't contract an involuntary Elvis impersonation, I'm doing just fine. Thank you. Thank you very much.

How to Lose Weight
and Make Money

A seven-year study at Johns Hopkins University examined the relationship between music and the consumption of food. Scientists counted bites and chews and concluded that people eat more slowly and consume less while listening to soothing, tranquil music. This may not disturb you, but other facets of the study should. Subjects in the study who dined on a full-course lunch to the strains of "The Stars and Stripes Forever" gulped an average of 5.1 bites per minute for a total eating time of thirty-one minutes. (Don't ask me how much 0.1 bite is. Maybe it's what stays stuck in your teeth.) Nearly half of the participants wanted seconds. The same was true for raucous rock 'n' roll tunes. Diners who listened to flute instrumentals consumed only 3.2 bites per minute.

smaller, consuming their meal took almost an hour, and no one asked for more food. People eating without music finished their meal in 40 minutes, taking 3.9 bites per minute.

Anyone who watches television has probably seen the ridiculous parade of products, e.g., Gutbuster, Abdominizer, Belly Burner, and Fat Frier, marketed to lure unsuspecting couch potatoes onto their feet to dial a toll-free number to buy a product they'll stop using a day after the money-back guarantee expires. Imagine that. While we've been spending large sums of money on various weight loss contraptions, there has been a simple solution right under our batons: don't play Sousa marches during meals.

You might even consider playing recordings in the concession stand.

I suppose John Philip Sousa would be disturbed to know that his marches are contributing to uncontrollable weight gain. He probably would also be perturbed to hear his marches mentioned in the same breath (or should I say mouthful) as rock 'n' roll. But on the flip-side, flute players are certainly very pleased with the study. I'm sure it's only a matter of time before flute players are putting out weight loss

CDs, cassettes, and videos with inviting titles like "Losing Fat with Flutes", "Rampal's Losing Pounds with Pierre" (in England that would have a double meaning), or possibly "Getting Lighter the Easy Way with Galway".

What does this mean to the band directing profession? Plenty. And not all of it is bad news. We can actually lose weight *and* make money. Take football game concession stands, for example. If your band receives proceeds from the concession stand, it would serve you well to crank up some Sousa marches and just watch the accelerando of bites and chews as thousands of spectators eat faster and then return for seconds of those band pickles, hot dogs, nachos, popcorn, and other goodies. I figure that playing "Belle of Chicago", "El Capitan", "The Fairest of the Fair", and "The Stars and Stripes Forever" at each home football game (let's say with an attendance of 3,000 people and an average eating time of five minutes) will increase total bites from about 58,500 to 76,000. Assuming these folks go back for seconds because they finished so quickly, you're looking at major food sale increases. You might even consider playing recordings in the concession stand and complete this subliminal frenzy by naming various items after Sousa marches —

King Cotton Candy, The Capitan Burger, Liberty Bell Pizza, Washington Post Pickles, etc.

As is often the case, questions arise whenever a new study is released. What would happen if the music were a flute arrangement of a Sousa march? Would people lose their appetites when listening to saxophone quartets? Do tuba ducts make people want to stick their faces in a big juicy watermelon and have juice dribble down their chins? Do Schoenberg pieces cause the urge to eat at least twelve separate items on a typical visit to the refrigerator? Can anyone possibly chew fast enough to keep up with Holsinger's "Graysondance"? Would the music of various Italian masters ruin a Chinese dinner? Do jazz tunes make you chew food with uneven jaw movements? Should people stop watching marching bands at Thanksgiving parades so they don't overload on turkey and dressing?

Scientists should continue their fascinating studies. In the meantime, I'll be at the store looking for Sousa marches, speakers for the concession stand, and flute recordings to play at dinner.

Signs of
the Times

We live in a very litigious society where lawsuits are filed at the slightest of provocations. Several years ago a little old lady won a huge judgment against McDonald's when she burned herself with a cup of coffee. Apparently the hot coffee spilled when she placed the cup between her legs while receiving her change at the drive-through window. Cases like this have resulted in industry efforts to put warning labels on almost every conceivable item.

For instance, I received a basketball goal for Christmas, and while reading the assembly instructions, I noticed that there was a dire warning every other paragraph. I never realized putting a basketball goal together was so dangerous. The front

page   warns: *Follow   all*
instructions   carefully.   The
system may fall over without
weight in the base and could
cause serious personal injuries
such as broken bones, cuts,
nerve damage, paralysis, brain
injury, or death. Then it adds
the worst fate of all: *possible*
property   damage.   A   later

**. . . music
educators and
the music
industry need
to wake up !!**

warning cautions players to keep their faces away from
the net because *serious dental injury can occur if teeth
come into contact with the net.* I guess you can never be
too careful. So much for sticking my tongue out like
Michael Jordan when I'm dunking the ball.

That being said, I think music educators and the
music industry need to wake up. We have been slow to
recognize musical dangers and properly warn our
students and parents. I have yet to see a warning label
on any music products. Until the music industry
catches up with the times, band directors will have to
take up the slack by putting their own warning labels
on the appropriate sources of unspeakable danger.

There are a number of items I see as potential
hazards. Take marching bass drums, for instance. Last
marching season I made the mistake of helping one of

my bass drum players carry his instrument back to the bandroom one evening after a rehearsal. Being a brass player, I had never done that before. In five short minutes I gained new respect for all bass drummers and pregnant women alike. I thought my back was going to break. The following warning would be

appropriate for bass drums: *Carrying this instrument for extended periods of time can cause general discomfort and back pain. When marching backward at fast tempos, players may trip and crush unsuspecting band members.*

Other instruments merit warnings also. In fact, just about any instrument is an accident waiting to happen . . .

Flutes should carry this warning on their cases: *This instrument can cause dizziness. Do not play while operating a vehicle or heavy machinery.*

Trombones should also come with warning labels: *When played for extensive time periods, player's right arm may feel as if it is going to fall off. Also, when extremely bored, players of this instrument may trip fellow band members with their slides.*

Trumpets might have a note of caution: *Players who develop the ability to play high notes on this instrument may suffer from major head swelling.*

When thrown at high speeds, this baton can severely maim . . .

Snare drums should carry these words of caution: *Playing this drum destroys brain cells and renders a student totally incapable of keeping up with mallets, music, or other percussion items.*

Oboe and bassoon reeds should have the following written on their containers: *This item, when damaged or worn (real or imagined), can cause poor intonation or severe pressure in the head and can become the scapegoat for many other problems.*

Saxophones also carry inherent dangers: *When playing "The Barney Song" at extremely high dynamic levels, saxophones can cause headaches and nausea in parents and directors. Students, however, are immune.*

On euphonium cases, a warning similar to the following would suffice: *This instrument should never be called a baritone. Doing so can cause severe mental trauma in sensitive euphonium players.*

There are other items around the bandroom that pose unexpected dangers. For example, batons, objects often subject to the wrath of frustrated band directors, should carry a mini-label listing the risks to students: *When thrown at high speeds, this baton can severely maim inattentive band members.* It might also list a 1-800 number where a disgruntled director can purchase a Nerf® baton.

Band towers and podiums should include warnings like the following: *When throwing a temper tantrum on this item, do not fall off. Any fall can cause broken bones, embarrassment, and possible footage for television's "America's Funniest Home Videos".*

Music stands need stickers posted: *When raising this stand, the top may fly off causing severe cuts, abrasions, and worse yet, the destruction of continuity during a rehearsal.*

I'm sure there are many other accidents waiting to happen; unfortunately, we'll just have to discover those as they occur. By the way, turn the pages of this book very carefully. You may get a paper cut. Don't say I didn't warn you.

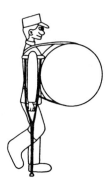

Excuses, Excuses

Students are notorious for their use of excuses. However, band directors are rather adept at the practice as well. Inexperienced band directors would do well to study the following list in order to keep up with their more experienced colleagues.

MARCHING SEASON
Our performance tonight was poor because...

...the publishers didn't put out any decent music this year.

...my drum major eloped with my only snare drummer.

...concert band is really my thing.

...this is a young group.

...half of the band came down with the chicken pox.

...I inherited students who didn't even know how to put their horns together correctly.

...my majorettes and their mothers went on strike.

...it rained on Monday, hailed on Tuesday, sleeted on Wednesday, and the temperature reached 110 degrees on Thursday.

...my trumpet soloist forgot his instrument.

...my bass drummer carries the melody on the closer and he broke his leg playing touch football with other band members.

...we had national standardized tests every day during band class.

CONCERT SEASON
Our performance was poor because...

...our football team made the play-offs and we marched four extra ballgames.

...we had four assemblies during our rehearsal time this week alone.

...I get no support from the administration.

...even my sophomores have senior-itis.

...my piccolo player missed the bus.

...the band budget is too small.

. . . my whole trombone section is academically ineligible.

...kids just aren't like they used to be.

...marching band is really my thing.

...my whole trombone section is academically ineligible.

...the percussion section brought the wrong music.

...we spent too much time selling fruitcake, candy, light bulbs, and toothbrushes—no time to rehearse.

Gaining
Perspective

One of the challenges all directors face is objectively assessing the performances of their bands. After receiving disappointing ratings, directors often fail to grasp why their performances were scored so low. They struggle to understand just what judges heard (or in the case of marching band, saw) that would cause them to rate the performances the way they did.

There are several reasons for this. First, it's easy to become so emotionally wrapped up in the process of contest preparation—how hard the kids have worked, how hard *you* have worked, etc.—that there is a tendency to hear what you want to hear and, in the case of marching bands, see what you want to see.

Secondly, immediately after a contest it is rather easy to be very forgiving of your own band's mistakes. Thirdly, we like to compare our performance with those of other bands, concluding that we were shortchanged because we were as good as or better than another band at the contest. Finally, I believe that human nature urges us to blame someone else for our own shortcomings.

There are several things that can be done to avoid these pitfalls. To avoid getting too wrapped up in your group's performance, you must find some way to gain some distance or perspective on your performance *before* you enter a contest. Have several respected colleagues guest conduct the band and offer constructive criticism and a frank evaluation of your band's performance. One of the guest clinicians should become involved early enough to be a part of your initial attempts to formulate and teach logical interpretations of the works you are performing.

It is also important to listen to recordings of your group after contests, not just immediately afterwards, but several months or, better yet, a year later. It's amazing what a little time will do. I remember the disappointment early in my career when my fine eighth grade band received a rating lower than expected. We played a very difficult program, and I thought we should have received more recognition for that in the scoring. But now I listen to the recording and wince at some of the problems we had. I now understand that all contest music should be performed well; judges rarely give points for a mediocre performance of difficult music.

Funky Winkerbean cartoon reprinted with special permission of North America Syndicate.

When evaluating a recording, it is important to note positive aspects as well as shortcomings; the good points indicate what you should continue to do. Watch videos of marching performances several months after marching season is over. Find areas of improvement and make a commitment not to repeat errors from the previous year. This distance allows you to note things that at the time maybe did not seem so bad but with distance seem excruciating. If you do this enough, you will eventually be less hasty in criticizing judges' comments and ratings.

Although we will inevitably compare our ensemble with others at a contest, comparisons should be de-emphasized because they are of little positive value. Strive to make the most of your band's potential without dwelling on how your score compared with that of another band. When possible, hold up the performances of outstanding bands as worthy of respect and emulation. Find recordings of your contest selections performed by outstanding ensembles. These are the comparisons that are worthwhile; compare yourself to the best and shoot for the stars.

Finally, avoid the blame game. Constantly blaming judges sends the wrong messages to students. Still greater harm is caused by more outward displays of displeasure. Stories abound of ungrateful directors and, unfortunately, their impressionable students who toss their second place marching trophies in the trash, stomp on the judges' cassette tapes, lambaste the judging, etc. As a coach of my daughter's basketball team, I try not to blame the referee every time we lose. There are plenty of things we as a team can correct before we go blaming someone else. Blaming others keeps us from growing and causes us to miss opportunities to teach our students valuable lessons—

how to handle disappointment with class, the importance of working together towards a goal, having a winning attitude and work ethic regardless of the contest results, and many others.

Directors who consistently fault judges only show their inexperience or incompetence. It is inappropriate (and unwise) for a first year director to severely criticize a judging panel with more than forty years of combined experience. Judges may make mistakes, but generally they deserve credit for doing a difficult job.

Although it is tempting to think only the best of our ensembles, we should work to overcome our first reactions and strive to gain a realistic perspective of each performance so the next will be better than the last.

Learning from Contest Comments

At many marching and concert contests, adjudicators will tape record their comments about each band. After the event, directors can simply listen to these tapes to find a way to improve their groups, but there are some techniques to use the evaluations more effectively.

Preview the tapes to select the most useful material for students so only one class period will be spent on the reviewers' comments. After students have listened to the most pertinent sections, ask them to write the five most helpful comments and five that seem of little use. This exercise will reflect what students perceive as irrelevant or important aspects of a good performance. At some point it may help to discuss how some adjudication comments that seem petty at first will gain significance later. A videotape of the performance will illustrate some comments students may not understand or agree with.

Focus the students' attention on important musical concepts such as tone quality, balance, dynamic contrast, intonation, phrasing, tempo, and rhythmic precision. For comments concerning marching, call attention to any mention of posture, carriage, intervals, alignment, and other fundamentals. Ask students to write down comments that were mentioned at least three times by the judges.

> **Students should write down five things that they personally are doing well.**

After the discussion period, students should write down five things that they personally are doing well and five things they could improve on to make the band better. These comments will reflect how effectively the discussion communicated ideas to the group.

These techniques can be supplemented by watching and evaluating videotapes of other bands. Bands that lack a marching tradition can watch tapes of excellent groups to understand what is possible; a videotape of a band with similarities of size and instrumentation would be most beneficial.

When concert season rolls around, adapt these procedures to recordings by other ensembles of pieces you are rehearsing or performing. Compare and contrast the balance, tone quality, intonation, tempo, style, and other musical factors. To ensure that students take these activities seriously, grade the assignment.

By assessing performances together, students and directors can find effective solutions to improve performance skills, concentration, and the ability to listen critically.

Top Ten Reasons to
Become a Band Director

#10 Genuine excitement on Friday nights and most Saturdays.

#9 Weight loss at marching practices where the temperature hovers around 100 degrees.

#8 Leadership and sales experience peddling fruit, candy, calendars, chili, toothbrushes, magazine subscriptions, pizza, and other assorted items.

#7 Trips to places all over the country (while supervising several dozen kids).

#6   Exciting mail on a daily basis.

#5   Free demo tapes and CDs.

#4   The mental stimulation of drill
      design.

#3   Complimentary concert folders,
      pens, and note pads from music
      companies.

#2   Freebies at conventions.

**AND THE #1 REASON FOR BECOMING A BAND
DIRECTOR . . .**

Less money per hour than most of
your students make ! !

All I Need to Know
I Learned in Beginning Band

Robert Fulghum's *All I Need to Know I Learned in Kindergarten* makes the point that rules for living are pretty basic and remain constant throughout life. It's much the same with music: fine performances by even the greatest ensembles are simply an extension and outgrowth of basics we all learned in a beginning class. Here is my list:

> Be on time to rehearsal.
> Sit up straight.
> Look at the time signature.
> Look at the key signature.
> Take a big breath together.
> Start together.
> Count.

Watch the director while you play.
Listen.
Always do the best you can.
Don't give up.
Play with feeling.
Don't puff your cheeks.
End together.
Take pride in what you have learned and
    accomplished.
Don't hit your neighbor with a mute or
    drumstick.
Practice.
Clean your instrument regularly.
Protect your reeds.
Be able to laugh at yourself.
Tell your parents about the next concert.

Bad Day at the Office

Today was not a good day. It was the last day of a month I would like to forget. Don't get me wrong. I love my job. It's just like with everything else in life— there are ups and downs. And today was down.

It all started at 5:15 a.m. when the phone rang. It was Donna Sue McPhearson, a band parent whose main goal in life is to ask me as many questions as possible.

"Did I wake you up?" she asked, not really caring to hear the answer. I managed a Neanderthal-type grunt before she continued. "I'm sorry, but I was calling to see what time the kids will be returning from their trip on Friday."

"You should have gotten an itinerary last week."

"That Cassandra! What am I going to do with her? She never brings anything home."

"We mailed it out."

"Oh . . . that must have been what Brutus, our rottweiler, chewed up last week along with part of the mail carrier's pants leg. The fabric and paper were so mashed up together we couldn't read anything. Cassandra told me the band would be back from the trip at 10:00 p.m., but I just wanted to be sure."

"It *is* 10:00 p.m."

She also went on to discuss how she would like to throw a Tupperware® party for the band to raise money. I agreed to do it next month just so I could get ready for work.

Funky Winkerbean cartoon reprinted with special permission of North America Syndicate.

Since I had early duty, I hurriedly took my kids to their school, rushed to my office, threw down my brief case, and reported to my assigned area. At about

7:45 a.m., a fight erupted between two students big enough to star for the WCW Wrestling Federation. Like Batman and Robin, the junior high director and I broke it up. He sustained slight injuries after being hit by a club. I was unscathed. After filling out the three page Discipline Report Form 103978B and four page Personal Injury Witness Report Form 15472A, I headed to the band room.

> **"How much money did you make at your last fund-raiser?" "THREE MILLION DOLLARS."**

When I arrived at my office, I could see a perky fund-raising representative posted at my office door. The last thing I wanted to see that early was a fund-raising rep, much less one who's disgustingly chipper.

I had barely managed a grunt acknowledging his presence when he asked, "How much money did you make at your last fund-raiser?"

Thinking I might discourage him, I exaggerated slightly, "Three million dollars."

Undaunted, he replied, "Want to make four million?" After a ten-minute talk, I agreed to sell waffle irons the next month so I could start first period.

Finally I could teach. This is what I was born to do. I'm not here to break up fights or sell everything under the sun. Just teach. My arms made their descent, ready to draw forth a glorious—

Beep. Beep. It was the intercom. "Let me have your attention for the morning announcements." Five minutes later I began again—

Beep. Beep. "Mr. Reely. Could you please send Bubba Henson to the office? He needs to get his lunch money." Gritting my teeth, I murmured a firm, "Yes."

I ignored all other beeps as we immersed ourselves in the music. The phone rang. I ignored it. Ten minutes later an office worker came in.

"Mr. Reely, the principal needs to see Bubba in the office." Needless to say, Bubba was not a popular fellow at that moment. I eyed him warily as he sheepishly exited the room. His friends told me he hit someone on the bus with his trombone.

After first period came mercifully to a close, another fund-raising rep appeared in my office doorway. Somehow I had missed that it was National Fund-raiser Day.

"How much money did you make with your last fund-raiser?"

"Four million."

"How would you like to make five million? This won't take much of your time..."

After a thirty minute presentation, I agreed to sell bubble bath next month . . . free Barney doll with every five sold. At least I'll get a relaxing bath out of the deal.

After I finished second period roll call, an office worker brought me a note. "Please dismiss all students for an assembly today. Sorry for the late notice. At the last minute we had the opportunity to see a traveling mime troupe do their version of *Evita*."

> "How would you like to make five million? This won't take much of your time..."

Third period was a pep rally. Everything went fine except for the fact that our bari sax player dropped his instrument off the top bleacher while doing the macarena.

I was actually able to teach for ten minutes during fourth period before a fire drill sent us outside into the 110 degree heat for twenty minutes.

I dropped into my chair as fifth period began. Finally, my prep period. Knock. Knock. Another fund-raising rep walked up to my desk.

"How much did you make in your last fund-raiser?"

By this point I was a fund-raiser's dream. "Where do I sign?"

"Right here, sir. And thank you for supporting Coconuts, Inc., from Hawaii. See you next month!"

Maybe leaving the office would help. I had just enough time to make some copies in the teacher workroom before lunch. Out of order. I went to the senior high library. After waiting in line for ten minutes, it was my turn. I only needed twenty copies of a quiz. After the nineteenth copy the copier jammed. An error code number appeared that I had never seen before. After filling out Repair to District Equipment Form 69429C, I went to lunch.

As I sat down to eat, the telephone rang in the dining area. A colleague answered. "Mr. Reely, it's for you. It's Galactica Tour and Travel Consultants or something like that."

"Hello."

"Mr. Reely? Would you like to take your band on a space shuttle mission this summer?"

"Do I have to go, too?"

"Yes, since you're the director."

"Then I'm not interested. Thank you."

After lunch I had five minutes, so I decided to read a couple of short chapters of *Don't Sweat the Small Stuff*, a book that I find helps me keep things in perspective. I couldn't find it . . . must have left it at home.

During sixth and seventh periods, I had to help proctor a standardized test given to the whole school. With a concert coming up next week, the missed rehearsals really hurt.

After a couple of after-school lessons, I waited thirty more minutes until the last student's parent showed up. As I was locking the bandroom door, I felt a tap on my shoulder.

A smartly dressed woman with a briefcase asked, "Are you the band director?"

"Sometimes I wonder," I replied, heading toward my car. Seeing her puzzled look I added, "Just kidding. I made five million dollars in our last fundraiser."

"That's amazing! What did you sell?"

"Rat poison. They say it tastes great. Rats eat it up."

"I think you better stick with that. I don't think I could help you raise but about $10,000."

Either this gal was a rookie or just plain honest. As I was closing my car door, I felt a twinge of guilt and told her, "Whatever you're selling, we'll sell it next month. Send me a contract."

A fitting end to a bad day. I guess I could say it's been a bad month, but I'm looking on the bright side. After all, the down times make me appreciate the up times. It's a new day tomorrow. I can just start over. In fact, it's a whole new month. Next month couldn't possibly be as bad as this one.

Move Over
Mr. Holland

The success of the film *Mr. Holland's Opus* will surely bring on more films concerning band and orchestra directors in the future. I humbly offer some titles and plots for movie directors to consider.

Mr. Holland's Opus 2. Richard Dreyfuss returns as a fund-raising representative. Through his efforts JFK High School sells enough grapefruit to salvage the band, orchestra, and drama programs and hire three more athletic coaches.

Mr. Holland's Opus 3. Richard Dreyfuss, now a millionaire, loses all the money he has in a lawsuit filed by the parents of his former student Rowena, alleging that he encouraged her to go to New York where she almost died from a street mugging.

Cueless. An inexperienced band loses its director to stomach ulcers just before a big contest but gives an inspired performance under the leadership of a student conductor.

Dead Man Marching is the story of an unfortunate first-year band director who receives a third division rating in marching band after the previous band director had 25 years of straight first divisions.

Silence of the Flams. Drummers in a local high school band suddenly begin disappearing as the bass drummer mysteriously gets fatter.

The Phantom profiles the mysterious crusader who hides band books, music, instruments, mutes, and other personal items from unsuspecting band students.

Mission Impossible. Tom Cruise portrays a first year band director who tries unsuccessfully to get his ten alto saxes to play in tune.

A Time to Kill. Tom Cruise returns as a second year band director who turns to other alternatives.

Waiting to Exhale tells the story of a marching band alternate who eagerly awaits the opportunity to march in his first ballgame.

Cutthroat Island. A first year band director struggles to survive on a tropical island while being pursued by three former state contest judges.

Mortal Combat. An action thriller starring Jean-Claude Van Damme as a band director defending himself against majorette mothers.

Flirting with Disaster. Band director with a poor oboe player performs two Rossini transcriptions at concert festival.

Drum and Drummer chronicles two drummers' three-year search to discover a new rudiment only to find that their discovery was already called the paradiddle.

Field of Screams. At the prompting of a mysterious voice saying, "Put up the tent and they will come," a retired circus band director puts up a circus tent in his cornfield so he can play circus screamers to huge audiences.

While You Were Sleeping. A percussionist's narcolepsy causes him to miss an entire symphony concert while on stage.

Thin Line Between Love and Hate is the story of a band director who struggles to get his band's double reeds to play in tune.

Sudden Death. A futuristic thriller where bands at marching contests break ties by marching the show again and stopping at their first mistake.

Dangerous Minds. Documentary exploring what percussionists do while bands work on slow concert band pieces requiring no percussion.

Rocky XXX. Sylvester Stallone returns as an itinerant boxer using his family troupe to provide shameless boxing matches for band fund-raisers.

Jaws XXX. A band encounters a sea disaster while taking a cruise to the Bahamas for the All-Caribbean Band Festival. Alto saxes save the day by playing a quartet and scaring the great white shark away.

To Die For. A morbid first year band director of a fifteen piece junior/senior band performs (mutilates) *March to the Scaffold, Come Sweet Death,* and *Death and Transfiguration* at a concert festival.

Homeward Bound 3 (The Incredible Journey). Three clarinet players in a 300-piece marching band get lost during a half-time show, but because of heroic efforts and quick thinking, they make it back to their spots before the closer.

Behind the Times
and Losing Ground

It seems like only yesterday that I was a junior in high school, rummaging around in our band's sound room preparing for a party to be held after our Friday night football game when I discovered dozens of band demo records. As my finger followed titles like "Disco Inferno," "Sgt. Pepper's Lonely Hearts Club Band," and "The Love Boat," I felt as if I had discovered hidden treasure. So *this* is how band directors selected our music for the upcoming fall! Not being a particularly bright child, I had not given the matter much thought previously, but the discovery was exciting nonetheless. I asked the band director if I could take them home and listen to them. He agreed to my request but probably regretted it later as I suggested my personal favorites for future performances.

Twenty years and hundreds of demo recordings later, I still get excited each spring when the new demo recordings arrive. Each year when the marching demos come, I receive odd looks from fellow faculty members as I skip down the hall, arms outstretched, proclaiming "They're here! They're here!"

Okay, I'm exaggerating, but I still have a strong interest in the latest arrangements for marching band. Unfortunately, choosing music is not as easy as it appeared when I was a student. As a fledgling director, my trumpet sections struggled with anything above the staff or faster than quarter notes. It was rather hard to find exciting arrangements they could actually perform.

Even as my bands have improved, the process seems to get no easier. How in the world can a band director hopelessly behind the times select music to please today's younger generation? One year a group of my hard-rockers got hold of a marching CD and went crazy over an arrangement of a tune called "Iron Man" by a group called Black Sabbath. Just their enthusiasm alone was enough to scare me.

Even titles are confusing now. One recent number one hit was a selection called "Tubthumping" by a group called Chumbawamba. I have never thumped a tub (at least knowingly, anyway), and I think I saw a Chumbawamba at the Memphis Zoo a couple of years ago in a South American marsupial exhibit.

> I receive odd looks from fellow faculty members as I skip down the hall, arms outstretched, proclaiming, "They're here! They're here!"

Confusion mounts as I contemplate using music by other groups with destructive names like Smashing Pumpkins, Crash Test Dummies, and Smash Mouth. Could you have imagined this trend in the past? We would have had groups like the Smashed Platters, Buddy Holly and the Crushed Crickets, DDT and the Beatles, the Drowned Monkees, Peter, Paul, and Mashed Mary, and other violent monikers.

The irony of the situation is that as I get older and more hopelessly out-of-date, I am simultaneously becoming more hip. With the advent of cable television and renewed interest in the oldies, my students are actually enjoying some of my music. Imagine my excitement when students nod their heads approvingly to the music of my teenage years, performers like

Earth, Wind, and Fire, Styx, Elton John, Billy Joel, and Chicago.

I have to admit, though, that I can't name a top ten hit from the last fifteen years unless it has been arranged for band or I just happen to remember it from glancing at a top ten chart in the Wal-Mart music section. I do take some consolation in the fact that my band students enjoy listening to band demo recordings with the same enthusiasm I did twenty years ago. Maybe if we combine my determination of what's right musically with their judgment of what is cool, everyone will be happy each marching season.

Things We'd Like to Hear

Have you ever caught yourself saying, *"Just once I'd like to hear..."* Well, the following is a list of things I think we *all* would like to hear.

From the administration:

"I like this budget proposal. Are you sure you don't want more?"

"I guess we'll have to hire another band director to help you guys out."

"What time is your concert tonight?"

From the guidance counselor:

"An All-State tuba player is moving into our district. Is it too late to put him in band?"

"None of your band students has scheduling problems this semester. "

"Six of your beginners next year have parents on the school board."

From the football coach:

"The band sounded great tonight. Thanks for your support."

From my doctor:

"I think we can reduce your intake of Maalox to one bottle a day."

From the parents:

"Thank you."

"Is there anything I can do to help?"

"I can chaperone any trip you need me."

"Could you play another work by Holst?"

From the students:

"Yes, sir."

"Thank you."

"You're a cool band director."

"I can't wait until our next fund-raiser!"

"I love scales. Can you teach me some more?"

"Is two hours a day enough practice?"

"Do you have a Beethoven CD I can borrow?"

"I've finished my Arban book. Do you have some more trumpet books?"

"It was my fault."

"I don't want to play 'Louie Louie' anymore."

"Is there anything I can do to help?"

"Can I come to the concert early tonight?"

"What! No chorale in warm-up today?"

"I only have four reeds that are playing properly. Could you sell me another box?"

"Can we have a sectional after school today?"

"I cleaned my instrument last night."

"All the fund-raising money is in on time."

"Lip slurs and long tones really are fun."

"My parents are buying me my own tuba."

"I went ahead and fixed all the music stands. I hope you don't mind."

"This parade is too short."

"Ninety-five degrees? No problem."

"I can only perform in three solo and ensemble events?"

"Can we play a Sousa march?"

"Can we do that *one more time*?"

Sorry Charlie!

A quality shared by my favorite teachers is the ability to take life's experiences and use them as illustrations to help students grasp concepts they might otherwise misunderstand or soon forget. I have tried to emulate that quality in my own teaching, and I am always on the lookout for a vivid example. One of my favorites is a true story I use to illustrate the proper concept of breathing.

I had many animals during my childhood—hamsters, gerbils, dogs, pigeons, and fish. This would make extended vacations quite difficult at times. During the summer of 1971, my family spent the summer at Fort Walton Beach while my Dad trained at a local Air Force Base for his tour in Vietnam. As final preparations were being made for the trip, my dad turned his attentions to the transportation of my personal menagerie. He entered my room carrying an old, white bucket and a long, clear tube.

"What's that for?" I asked.

"We're going to siphon the water out of the aquarium," he replied matter-of-factly.

My suspicions rising a little, I queried further, "Won't it hurt the fish?"

"No, they'll know better than to come near the tube." Having said that, he lowered one end of the tube into the water. My doubts soon mingled with curiosity since I had never seen anything siphoned before. Dad put the opposite end of the tube into his mouth and inhaled very quickly. As the water began its journey through the tube, Charlie, one of my pet goldfish, exhibited a little curiosity of his own. I looked on in growing terror as Charlie swam toward the tube, and before you could say "Go fish!" the tube had sucked out Charlie's left eyeball. My body convulsed as the eyeball wound its way through the long tube before summarily plopping into the bucket. By this point, my Dad realized that he had grossly overestimated the intelligence of my goldfish.

Fortunately, Charlie lived. A glass eye was out of the question, and the pet store didn't have any miniature eye patches so Charlie had to be content with a relatively large cavity on the side of his head (considering his low IQ I'm not sure he noticed). Other than an occasional bump into the side of the aquarium he continued to live a happy life for another year. Charlie became the hit of the neighborhood. I was able to give mini-tours to friends who wanted take a gander at Charlie the One-Eyed Goldfish.

If Charlie was still alive, he would be proud to know that his tragedy also provided the perfect illustration for suction—the best description of how air is brought into the body before playing a wind instrument. Students should pull air into their bodies before they play in the same way that the tube sucked in Charlie's eyeball.

Is this illustration a little off-the-wall and bordering on gross? Yes and maybe. Is it vivid and, pardon the expression, eye-popping? Certainly. That's what every important concept needs—a memorable illustration. Use interesting stories to illustrate certain musical concepts and you'll find that your students grasp concepts quicker, retain them longer, and even have a little fun in the process.

How to Succeed in Band
(without really trying)

Like personal hygiene and good table manners, practicing at home can be traumatic for junior high school musicians. The following practice tips, supplied by several third clarinetists and two bassoon players, are sure to motivate even the most uninspired students.

General Suggestions

Never practice when your home is completely quiet. At least turn on the TV, stereo, or washing machine—anything that will help you avoid extended musical concentration.

Position your music in a manner that allows for a relaxed playing position (good posture is something you only use in band rehearsal). If you like to snack while practicing, fasten your music to the refrigerator with bright vegetable-shaped magnets. Practicing in bed offers the opportunity for little naps between etudes. Another option is to place the music on top of the television set so you can practice without missing any of your favorite shows.

FUNKY WINKERBEAN   **Tom Batiuk**

Funky Winkerbean cartoon reprinted with special permission of North America Syndicate.

Only practice pieces you like and can already play with few mistakes. Save scales, technical exercises, rudiments, and technical passages for the night before a band test; that is the optimum time to practice.

Never use a metronome; it will inhibit expression, particularly on scales and arpeggios.

Do not worry about practicing correct articulations and dynamics. It is the band director's job to tell you all that stuff in rehearsal (it makes him feel needed).

Do not take big breaths or practice at more than fifty percent of your capacity. Save your best stuff for performances when it's absolutely necessary.

Try to play immediately after meals before brushing your teeth. The interesting things growing in your instrument may qualify you for bonus points in science class.

Good practice sessions don't just happen; they require foresight, planning, and a thorough knowledge of prime-time programming. Here's an example of how to structure practice time so the student can avoid the trauma of musical success.

Practice Schedule

6:55   Get *TV Guide*.

7:00   Get out instrument. Do any maintenance such as oiling valves, applying cork grease, etc. This takes up at least three minutes and you still have not played a note.

7:03   Make sure you can see the music and the television.

7:05 Brass players should spend the next ten minutes playing the highest notes possible (do not waste time on warm-ups). Drummers should play as many funky rhythms as possible. If appropriate, drum along with the television show. Woodwinds should imitate as many different species of waterfowl as possible (this goes nicely with National Geographic specials).

7:15 Get down to serious practice during commercials, playing scales or rudiments you already can play accurately. Do not worry if you miss a note here or there; you're still playing some kind of scale that is sure to appear some time or another.

7:18 Play as many tunes from football season and past concerts as possible. For an extra challenge try them by memory.

7:30 If you are watching a half-hour television program, move to the bedroom for a change of pace (your family will thank you).

7:35 Call your best friends to catch up on all the latest news and ask them if they are practicing as hard as you are.

7:45 After a needed break, it is time to hit the hard stuff. Turn on the radio, lie down on the bed in a comfortable playing position, and work for fifteen minutes on the next day's band test.

8:00 Finally, take one last shot at hitting a few high notes before ending your practice session. Drummers should try to set new volume records while playing sixteenth notes at quarter note = 500.

After practicing, go back to uninterrupted television viewing. If nothing interesting is on TV, you can always do your homework.

Confessions of a Technically Handicapped Band Director

I have a confession to make. I am technically handicapped. You may wonder what that means and since there is no official definition that I know of, I'll define it myself:

technically handicapped: *1. completely lacking the motor skills necessary to adjust, repair, or construct anything with any marked degree of success; 2. in music, the inability to perform the simplest of adjustments and repairs on instruments without increasing complications and utter disaster; 3. mechanically impaired.*

There is no scientific data to confirm my suspicions, but I believe that I have been technically handicapped since birth. As a very young child, building a house out of blocks presented insurmountable difficulties. My creations generally resembled earthquake wreckage. My problems continued in elementary school as I tried to construct model airplanes. That confounded airplane glue stuck to anything and everything as my poor hands tried to apply it to those minuscule aviation parts. Resulting creations bore little resemblance to the pretty picture on the front of the box. In high school I spent one summer roofing houses and earned the nickname Mr. Lightning, because when I hammered in roofing nails, I never hit the same spot twice.

I masked my ineptitude for several years until it was time to student teach. The university I attended did not provide any repair classes (it would have only lowered my GPA anyway), and when my band director did take us to visit a repair shop, it only increased my fear of the future. Indeed, my concerns about student teaching were not centered around the actual teaching, but the fear that the supervising teacher or some student would hand me a broken horn and say, "Fix it." The possible scenarios my mind conjured up were worsened when I also realized that in trying to figure out the problem on one of my minor instruments, I might not be able to tell if the problem was the instrument or me!

Fortunately, there was another student teacher that was with me at the same school who played clarinet. Since I could delegate all woodwind repairs to her, that left me with the brasses and the remote possibility of percussion. It couldn't be too bad, at least brasses don't have all those doo-dads and gizmos you find on woodwind instruments.

After about a week of student teaching, I received my first challenge—a detached trumpet spit valve. I was a trumpet player so this seemed easy enough even though my own personal spit valves had never come off. But as I tried manipulating the little spring that returns the valve to the down position, it would slip from my hands and leap onto the worktable like a cricket. Through brute strength and pure determination, I was eventually victorious and proudly handed the humbled instrument back to its owner after a thirty-minute struggle.

My next task was learning how to use a Thompson mouthpiece puller. One look at it reminded me of medieval torture devices I had studied about in history class. I was convinced my hands were going to put some instrument through pure agony. After fumbling through all the old and worn crescent-shaped pieces and finding matching numbers, I placed the trumpet into the correct position. With each turn of the screw, I expected the whole instrument to collapse and squeak out a final high C. Fortunately, my fears were relieved as the puller did its job and the mouthpiece plopped onto the table.

Despite my fear of repairing instruments (fixophobia), I entered my first year of teaching determined to be Mr. Fix-it. Armed with my trusty  *Everything You Need to Know About Repairs* book, there was no challenge too great. Stuck mouthpieces and slides became tests of strength and manhood. Bent keys and springs tested my grace and finesse. Mysterious problems transformed me into a musical Sherlock Holmes, examining evidence and interrogating students to find the possible cause of an instrument's dysfunction.

In spite of this initial enthusiasm, my success rate was low and my blood pressure high, particularly on test days when half of the band miraculously had their instruments disintegrate simultaneously. Flute players with one note not responding could rest assured I would restore it, the only problem being that three other notes would be lost due to my adjustments. Replacing pads on clarinets usually resulted in burned fingers or a flaming instrument (the plastic ones just melted a little) as I attempted to apply the flame of a lighter against the key to secure a new pad. Springs on flutes snapped like dry pine needles before my very eyes. Once while trying to extract a mouthpiece from a tuba by hand (it was the macho thing to do), I didn't notice that the support between the leadpipe and the bell had become unsoldered. As I turned the mouthpiece, the leadpipe tubing rotated and bore a strong resemblance to a swirled licorice stick before I noticed the problem.

These mishaps took their toll, but the real breaking point came in a knock-down-drag-out struggle with one of the band's timpani that had an immovable pedal. Clutching my copy of *Timpani Repair for Dummies*, I approached the troubled timpani. My book stated: "If the pedal moves down when released, there is not enough tension in the spring. Tighten this by turning the tension control in a clockwise motion. If the pedal moves up when released, there is too much tension in the spring, so turn the knob in a counter-clockwise direction." Easy. Nothing to it. Just a little turn of the tension knob and . . . but as I looked at the pedal I realized that I was not really sure of what was up and what was down. Guessing the pedal was down, I decided to turn the tension rod clockwise. Nothing happened. Figuring that the pedal was not down after all, I turned the knob the other way. Concluding I was on the right track, I overzealously turned the knob one time too many, and the thing came out in my hand. Consequently, I spent the next thirty minutes trying to put the thing back where I got it.

I decided the timpani head was not as balanced as I had previously thought, so I removed the tuning lugs, counterhoop, and drum head and reset the drum to its fundamental pitch while pressing the pedal down (or was it up? I'm still confused!). As I prepared for the final test, I was hoping that once I reached the top pitch I could then return to the lower ones. I ascended slowly, and after reaching the top pitch, I nervously attempted to descend, only to find the pedal stuck again. In deep agony (it was no time to keep things in perspective) I fell to the ground, groveling for mercy in front of that cruel copper crucible. It was at this moment of deep despair that I resolved to become a full-time band director and leave repairs to a professional.

If you are technically handicapped, I suggest you get to know your nearest repair technician as soon as possible. If you suspect one of your colleagues is technically handicapped and needs professional help, but aren't quite sure, check the list on page sixty-eight for signs of this problem. Do this person a favor and give him a repair technician's card and tell him he is not alone.

In fact, there is historical evidence that several famous people in the arts were technically handicapped. Jean-Baptiste Lully (1632-1687) was probably technically handicapped. He hit his toe with the sharp point of a cane with which he was conducting, developed gangrene, and consequently died. It is my hypothesis that the high quality of Stradivarius violins diminished after Antonio's death in 1737 because all of his sons were technically handicapped. And then there is Vincent Van Gogh who cut off his ear with a Bic® disposable razor.

It is my hope that because of my confession other technically handicapped directors will step forward and no longer be ashamed of themselves. Maybe we should form a national organization and demand that instrument manufacturers construct instruments that have fewer parts, no little screws or wires, and the durability of cement. Until then, the technically handicapped will remain a lonely lot, struggling in silence to stay in the competitive world of music. I plan on sticking it out, but if things get too rough, I could always become a surgeon.

Sure Signs of a
Technically Handicapped Band Director

1.   Takes immeasurable pride in successfully oiling valves on brasses.

2.   Blames all woodwind problems on the reed.

3.   Cannot remember the names of tools (calls the pliers a wrench, etc.).

4.   Often injures himself and others trying to raise music stands.

5.   Has an office full of broken instruments with cobwebs forming.

6.   Has second degree burns on fingers from replacing pads.

7.   Sometimes says, "Let your dad fix it."

8.   Sometimes says, "Let the guy over at the pawn shop have a look at it."

9.   During marching season, has a percussion section with every member leaning forward and sideways at dangerous angles due to ill-fitting straps, harnesses, and braces.

Articles
That Inspire

When reflecting on my teaching experience, I often wonder what my students *really* think about music. Are they able to grasp its importance in spite of my inarticulate attempts to describe it? Do they feel its effects even when I falter and become obsessed with the process and not the product? I suppose one of the things that makes music alluring is, in fact, the mysterious hold it has on me, even though words are inadequate to fully describe just what music **is**. When I think of spending day after day teaching, prodding, and coaching (and having lots of fun), I sometimes question whether I imparted some essence of what music can mean in life. Were my students able to see by my example, my choice of career, that music is something to be cherished? Has music been able to overcome my inadequacies?

I like to collect books and videos on educational issues, and recently I read *Dangerous Minds,* a book that served as the basis for a movie. What impressed me most was the English teacher in the book who used a journal to understand the innermost feelings of her students. This enabled her to see issues from each student's point-of-view, thereby allowing her to take a more individualistic and understanding approach in her teaching relationships.

Keeping a band journal would be rather impractical, particularly in large band programs, but I have found an effective way to not only share my own thoughts about music with students but to gain insight from their perspectives as well. At one of the major exam times each year, I provide a magazine article to students and ask them to answer essay questions based on the article.

I have found three articles to be particularly suitable for this purpose. One is "Come Blow Our Own Horn" by William Hargrove (*Newsweek,* December 14, 1992). Hargrove, who started playing the saxophone at forty-three, gives his views on how music is perceived today. He laments the fact that Americans are spectators, not players, and encourages readers to learn an instrument and jam with friends just as others get together for pick-up basketball games. Reading this article hopefully helps students realize that being able to perform music is a gift they can enjoy long after high school. I ask questions like the following: "What do students at our school, in general, think about those involved in music? Why?" "What can our program do to help all students want to continue music study until they graduate from high school?" and "What avenues can you use to maintain your interest in music after you graduate?"

Another article I distribute to students, "The Cellist of Sarajevo, " (*Reader's Digest*, November, 1996) is a true story about Vedran Smailovic, a cellist with the Sarajevo Opera before the war, who for twenty-two days put on his full, formal concert attire, took up his cello, and walked into the midst of the battle. He sat in a chair next to a crater caused by a mortar shell and played Albinoni's Adagio in G Minor despite the bullets and bombs dropping around him. In response to the question "What do you believe the man was saying through his music?" one student responded, "I believe that he was saying that although they could break his body, they could not break the human spirit." "What did the author come to realize once he returned to his home in Maine?" evoked the following response:

"The author realized that music is a gift we all share equally, whether in war or a nursing home." To the question "Can music really unite people of different backgrounds, beliefs, ages, races, etc.? Why or why not?" one student commented, "Yes, music can unite us. We all share a common bond with each other, but sometimes it needs an extra link to bring us together. Music can be that link if we only let it."

In "The Goodness in Music" (*The Instrumentalist*, July, 1995), Robert Weirich looks for meaning in music and life after a heart-breaking car accident. His pregnant wife was hit by a drunk driver and the baby died. The responses to questions about this article were particularly meaningful. "What did Weirich conclude about ugly and senseless things that happen in the world?" elicited responses such as "He learned there is no making sense of it. It is simply there and threatens to engulf anyone who dwells on it too long. He has learned to respect its presence even as he focuses elsewhere." When I asked students to write what they thought Weirich meant when he wrote "There is more pain and far more joy in music than I had thought possible", one student responded, "I think that he realizes that music is more than words, sounds, and rhythms. He sees that music is a world all its own."

In response to the questions "Has music helped you in your life? Why or why not?" I have received some enlightening responses. One student commented, "Music has helped me through good times and bad. It helped me get over my father's death and has sometimes soothed my soul." Another answered,

> Music has given me a confidence in myself I never had before. Music has helped me to shed tears that I needed to cry. It has also helped me to find happiness. Music has given me something to focus on in life. It has provided a distraction when I needed one or an inspiring burst of creativity. Music has helped me gain trust from my friends and family. I know more people and have more friends through the music program than I could have anywhere else. The people that I am associated with through music accept me for who I am. Music and the people involved have taught me to keep going even when I wanted to give up.

It would be more than worth your effort to find these or other meaningful articles to present to your students during the year. Within the quiet exam period, students can find meaning in an inspiring article that says things in a way we cannot articulate. If you are like me, after reading their essays you will have learned more than they did.

"Yankee Doodle"
Mommy

In his book *Piano Pieces* Russell Sherman says that parents come in all temperaments and levels of sophistication. They can be crude, mute, or meddlesome. They can be deferential, enlightened, or gracious. They can be chronically angry or sweetly suffering . . . They can be positive reinforcers or negative scolds." While many parents I encounter through my work are gracious and positive reinforcers, every now and then I meet a parent who is indeed crude, chronically angry, and a negative scold. These parents generally think they know more about my job than I do.

Such was the case last year. It was the first week of school, and we were in the process of placing beginners on their instruments. We repeatedly emphasized to the kids (and parents via letters) that they should not buy a used instrument without bringing it in for us to examine. We also told them to use reputable dealers.

Despite this, one little girl brought a low quality flute to school that her mother had purchased despite our warnings. Unfortunately, we had encountered this brand before—cheap imitations made in China that are sold at major department stores and "versatile" mail-order companies specializing in cheap toys. We told her that the flute was of such low quality and poor condition that it would not be suitable. My colleague called the girl's mother that night to explain the situation. Things did not go well. Her six years in junior and senior high school band and weeks of watching "Lawrence Welk" reruns qualified her as an unequivocal expert in instrument manufacturing. She crudely dismissed his opinions and vowed to talk to the principal the next day.

True to her word, she stormed to the principal's office bright and early the next morning. After a short discussion, the principal referred her to our office where the fruitless conversation continued. I even tried to play the flute for her. Not even a simple tune like "Mary Had A Little Lamb" could be produced.

"That's funny," she said, "It was working last night. I played 'Yankee Doodle' on it. Here. Let me see that."

She proceeded to play a version of "Yankee Doodle" that was a compost heap of harmonic minor, Schoenberg twelve-tone, and Gregorian chant.

Keeping it simple, I asked her if she always played "Yankee Doodle" in a minor key.

"Yes, that's how we learned it," she replied.

Funky Winkerbean cartoon reprinted with special permission of North America Syndicate.

It was at this point that I realized reasoning with her was impossible. I tried to end the growing fiasco by simply stating that we want what's best for her daughter. If the instrument she had was a good quality instrument in playing condition, we had no problems whatsoever. If she wanted her daughter to make any kind of progress at all she would need another instrument. Local repair technicians would not even work on such an instrument of low quality.

After she spouted a few choice words we found rather insulting, she gathered her children and stormed out of our office chanting, "End of conversation! End of conversation!" like an old turntable with its needle stuck in a groove. Unfortunately, she was going to force her daughter to begin her musical studies on the useless flute they had purchased.

The junior director and I couldn't buy her a new flute, of course, but we decided to teach the best we could under the circumstances, showing the young flutist the respect and interest we would afford any other student. Despite our valiant efforts, however, the girl made minimal progress up until the time she moved to another town several weeks later. Undoubtedly, the "Yankee Doodle" mother told her daughter's new director about the scoundrels they had encountered at her previous school.

The ultimate difficulty in such situations is separating the student and her needs from the ignorance of the parent. It is tempting at times to dismiss the child when it is really the parent at fault. In such circumstances, we must step back and ask, "What's best for the child?" and act on the honest answer to that question.

Although not all attempts to convince parents of the answer to that question will be successful, playing

the role of child advocate can sometimes lead to a
change of heart on the part of the parents, keep the
child out of the middle, and give directors a clear
conscience for their efforts.

You Know It's Time
for a Vacation When . . .

Recognizing high stress levels is very important. Check out the following list. If too many things sound familiar, it may be time for you to get away from it all.

...you can feel your head pounding the tempo *before* the band begins to play.

...demo tapes for next year's marching season don't excite you.

...you use Rolaids® as a daily supplement to your diet.

...just the mention of the word "fund-raising" makes you ill.

...each class period seems as long as a Jerry Lewis telethon.

...a missed key signature in beginning band class almost gives you a nervous breakdown.

...you stare glassy-eyed at the Weather Channel until the wee hours of the morning.

...there's more hair on your hairbrush than your head.

...you can't remember the names of your spouse and kids.

...Funky Winkerbean cartoons don't make you laugh.

...all your batons are broken.

...you answer all questions with a frantic "No!" regardless of the question and sometimes even before they are asked.

...you go to work with clothes that don't match and you don't care.

...the difference between nightmares and reality becomes blurred.

...a Sousa march doesn't make you tap your foot.

...the thought of becoming an administrator becomes palatable.

...you watch "Mr. Rogers' Neighborhood" reruns to help yourself unwind.

...you sit in the teachers' lounge and gripe about your students.

...you have created a mountain of crumpled, partially completed drill charts and ask your four-year-old daughter if she would like to draw the next set.

...you begin to sympathize with those who commit violent crimes against humanity.

...your band is out-of-step and you don't care.

...you close your eyes at night and still see a drill design grid sheet.

...you learn of important news events weeks after they occur.

...you hide your oboe player's instrument.

...you have begun X-ing out each day on your desk calendar and have written **THE LAST DAY OF SCHOOL** in bold, capital letters within the appropriate date box.

Test Your
Musical Literacy

*In the wake of E.D. Hirsch's acclaimed book **Cultural Literacy** a number of books and articles emerged stating what the average American should know to be culturally literate. This quiz tests information Americans should know if they are to consider themselves musically literate.*

Multiple Choice (Correct answers—three points each.)

1. Rimsky-Korsakov was a:

    A.   Famous writing duo known for their popular musical, *Siberia!*

    B.   Russian weightlifter in the 1980 Olympics.

    C.   Russian composer of *Russian Easter Overture*.

    D.   Famous Latvian ballet dancer.

*C is correct. If you answered **B** you need to remember this is a music test.*

2. Yo-yo Ma is:

    A.   A quote from *Rocky IV*.
    B.   A corruption of the more derogatory "Yo mama".
    C.   Your mother's yo-yo.
    D.   A famous cellist.

    D is correct. If you chose A you may be right; I didn't feel like watching Rocky IV again to double check. Give yourself three points for A just in case.

3. Placido Domingo is a:

    A.   Beautiful capital of a Caribbean island.
    B.   Famous tenor.
    C.   New dish at Taco Bell.
    D.   Spanish clothes designer.

    B is correct. If you answered A check out a book on geography and deduct two points. If you chose C take a break for lunch.

4. Who began the British Invasion of America in 1964 with the hit "I Want to Hold Your Hand"?

    A.   The Beatles.
    B.   Hootie and the Blowfish.
    C.   Pavarotti.
    D.   Louis Armstrong.

    A is correct. If you answered C you need a review course in opera.

5. What is the Hollywood Bowl?

    A.   A New Year's Day football game sponsored by Hollywood Video.

    B.   A famous amphitheater in Los Angeles.

    C.   A prestigious music award.

    D.   A famous pro-am bowling event.

B is correct. If you chose A or D take a review course in sports trivia.

6. Is Elvis dead?

    A.   Dead as a door nail.

    B.   Last time I checked.

    C.   No way, I've seen him myself.

    D.   Elvis who?

Give yourself three points for any answer. There's no use stirring up more controversy.

7. Which of the following statements about the oboe is true?

    A.   An oboe is a band director's best friend.

    B.   The oboe is unjustifiably maligned in band and orchestra circles.

    C.   A poor oboe tone quality isn't so bad once you get used to it.

    D.   An oboe does not burn as long as a bassoon.

If you answered A, B, or C you are probably an oboe player. Give yourself three points for being a good sport. If you chose D count it right, but I would like some exact statistics to confirm this oft-heard assertion.

8. What problem did Beethoven encounter from 1798 until his death in 1827?

- A. Nagging wife.
- B. Mid-life crisis.
- C. Increasing deafness.
- D. Prolonged litigation over unauthorized use of his Symphony No. 5 in telephone answering machines.

C is the correct answer. If you chose D subtract two points; answering machines weren't invented yet.

9. What should you do at a band or orchestra concert in between movements of a multi-movement work?

- A. Clap boisterously and yell, "BRAVO".
- B. Run to the restroom.
- C. Cough.
- D Sit politely and wait for the next movement.

The best answer is D although A could be appropriate in rare instances. If you do choose to clap and yell make sure you are not the only one.

10. Rossini's *William Tell Overture* is better known as the theme to what famous television show?

- A. "Bonanza."
- B. "The Tonight Show."
- C. "The Brady Bunch."
- D. "The Lone Ranger."

D is correct.

11. Which of the following is the proper way to refer to the French horn?

    A.   French horn.
    B.   Horn.
    C.   Instrument with a hand rest.
    D.   Curvy thing with lots of tubes.

*The musically cultured answer is **B**. You may use **A**, however, when relating to less literate folk.*

12. Which is the correct way to refer to Handel's most famous work?

    A.   *Messiah.*
    B.   *The Messiah.*
    C.   *Miss Iowa.*
    D.   *Missouri .*

***A** is the acceptable answer, though you may want to use **B** like everyone else.*

13. Complete the words to the following song from Irving Berlin's *Annie Get Your Gun*. "Anything you can do, _____."

    A.   I can do better.
    B.   I cannot do at all.
    C.   I'd like to see it.
    D.   I probably could do it a little better if I felt like it and wanted to.

***C** is correct. If you selected **D** don't sell everything you own to become a lyricist.*

14. Complete the words to the following song: "That's the way, (Uh-huh-uh-huh), I like it, (___-___-___-___)".

    A.   Doo-wop-Doo-wop.
    B.   Ramma-lamma-ding-dong.
    C.   Mein Vater, Mein Vater.
    D.   Uh-huh-uh-huh.

D is the correct answer. If you answered C thinking that it was German lieder you are thinking much too hard. It's a hit song of 1975 by KC and the Sunshine Band.

15. Which of the following is **not** a song written by Stephen Foster?

    A.   "Camptown Races."
    B.   "Beautiful Dreamer."
    C.   "Don't Worry, Be Happy."
    D.   "Old Folks at Home."

C is correct. Foster did not write "Don't Worry, Be Happy" though there is some evidence he lived by that philosophy.

True-False (The point values for these items vary.)

16. I only listen to public radio broadcasts.

*If you answered **true** give yourself five points. If you regularly listen to country music subtract two.*

17. I still own all of my disco albums.

*If you answered **true** subtract three points. If you still have "Hooked on Classics" subtract one more. If you have purchased digitally remastered CD's of your disco albums subtract one more. If you answered **false** add five.*

18. The only classical recording I own is Beethoven's Symphony No. 5 in C minor.

*If you answered **true** give yourself one point, unless your Beethoven recording is a 78 record.*

19. I sing in the bathtub or shower.

*This is undoubtedly one of the most important signs of being musically literate. If you answered **true** give yourself ten points.*

Bonus Round (Give yourself one point for each of the following melodies you can hum.)

(a) "Eine Kleine Nachtmusik" by Mozart.

(b) "The Stars and Stripes Forever" by Sousa.

(c) "The Ballad of Gilligan's Island" by Wyle and Schwartz.

(d) "La donne é mobile" by Verdi.

(e) "The Ballad of Jed Clampett" by Scruggs

and Flatt.

(f) Any excerpt from a Schoenberg 12-tone composition.

(g) "Lassus Trombone" by Fillmore.

(h) Organ Fugue in G minor ("Little") by J.S. Bach.

Use the following scale to rate yourself:

SCORE	DESCRIPTOR
60 +	You are hopelessly cultured (musically at least).
40-59	Burn some of your disco albums.
20-39	Start singing in the shower.
0-19	Don't worry, be happy.

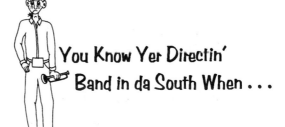

You Know Yer Directin' Band in da South When . . .

All regions of the United States have idiosyncrasies unique to their area, and the South is no different. I have spent all of my life in the South and have been able to experience these idiosyncrasies firsthand. This chapter takes a good-natured (and exaggerated) look at life as a band director in the South. I think it's interesting to note that I could not get any major periodicals to publish this because it was not politically correct. Sadly, they misjudged the ability of Southerners to laugh at themselves.

...most of your band kids show up for summer marching practices wearing cowboy boots and blue jeans.

...most of your instruments are held together with duct tape.

...your majorettes can out arm-wrestle the football team.

...your color guard buys uniforms to match their tattoos.

...your band parents boo the other band at halftime.

...there's more likely to be a can of Skoal than a mute in your first chair trumpet player's case.

...one of your students asks to play a GEETAR (guitar) in jazz band.

...essential equipment for band trips includes spit cups.

...most of your students wear baseball caps with their uniforms.

...most of your band boosters wear camouflage.

...your best fund-raiser is auctioning off a shotgun.

...your students think "motif" is what their grandparents need when they lose their dentures.

...half of your students skip a marching contest for a truck pull.

...your band booster president looks like Elvis.

...you sell snuff at the band concession stand.

...your band gets into fights with other bands after ballgames.

...your band parents make death threats to judges who give low scores.

...your halftime show includes themes from "Walking Tall."

...your superintendent doesn't understand why the new band uniform can't have a big belt buckle on it.

...it takes most of your band students longer to get to school than to an away football game.

...your students think Itzak Perlman is an awful mean fiddle player.

...your superintendent asks you to play more Johnny Cash tunes.

...your students think "adagio" is a common Italian word for canine.

...your flute section wears curlers on their legs before the prom.

...one of your tuba players bought a $3.97 cassette of "that Mossart dude's 'Einer Kleiner Notmusic.' "

...one of your senior bass drummers has a child in beginning band.

...your students believe the term "cantabile" refers to people who eat other people.

...the percussion section thinks you're talking to them when you mention the musical term "ritard."

...your students think "elegy" is what grows on the top of fishin' ponds.

...a band parent yells out "Way to play that tuber (tuba), Bubba!" after his solo during a concert band selection.

...your life is threatened after a chair test.

...jumper cables are kept on the dash of the school bus.

...several students offer to let you use their 4-wheel drive truck as a band tower.

...the students' truck stereos play louder than your band.

...your students refer to music played badly as "hearing the tune the ole cow died on."

...your students not only play in band but sing in the KWAR (choir).

...your keyboard players tell others that they play the BAILS (bells).

...your students go out "marchin' on the football FEEL (field)."

...the SPRANG (spring) sometimes comes off the KLARINET (pronounce AR as in CAR).

...your bus is late to an away game because it got behind a tractor.

...your students use the generic term "sodi" (pronounced So-DEE) for a soft drink, e.g., "I'm goin' over to Wal-Marts and buyin' me some tater logs and a sodi."

...you have to march in a Fourth of July parade.

...your students talk so slowly that rehearsal is over by the time one of them is finished asking one question.

...the first time your students ever heard of Beethoven was when they saw him as a puppy.

...you have to cancel a halftime show due to deer season.

...you need a knife for an emergency and fifty different kinds are offered by your brass section.

Bobby Jax

Students are memorable for various reasons, some good and some bad. Some we point to with pride, daring to take some of the credit for their success. Others serve as painful reminders of mistakes and lost opportunities. Still others stand out as inspirational lessons, drawing our ever-straying purpose back into focus with unmistakable clarity.

One of the battles I constantly face is the temptation to give up on a student too quickly, using my overrated experience to label a student as a potential "winner" or "loser." As our band program has grown and there are plenty of players to go around, the temptation is even greater. There's always someone to take a student's place, so the need to keep every kid is not so pressing as when the band was in its infancy.

The memory of one former band member helps me regain my focus when I am tempted to shortchange a student. Bobby Jax joined the Paragould band when he was in the seventh grade. Short, red-haired, and freckled, Bobby joined band with an excitement typical of beginners. He practiced each evening and proudly brought his battered and rusty trumpet to school each day. In fact, I think Bobby took his trumpet home after school every day for the six years he was in our program.

Bobby's progress was below average; his advancement being limited by his faulty embouchure that I tried to correct but to no avail. He auditioned for Junior High All-Region Band during his eighth and ninth grade years, finishing close to the bottom each time.

After three years as last chair in the junior high band, it was time for Bobby to move on to the senior high where matters became more complicated when he joined the marching band. His mistakes on the field are a part of Paragould band legend now, the most memorable being the time he fell backwards onto the seat of his pants at a halftime performance, spawning

an annual award that he good-naturedly accepted as
the first recipient.

Bobby tried out for both All-Region Concert
Band and All-Region Jazz Band his sophomore year
but did not make it. As region try-outs approached
during Bobby's junior year, I asked the band if anyone
would like some last minute help. I inwardly cringed
as Bobby raised his hand. Late that evening I sat in the
bandroom and gave Bobby a lesson as my five-year-old
son patiently sat by us until I finished "one more
lesson." With tired feet and
glassy-eyes from a long
day, I painfully sat through
missed rhythms, cracked
notes, and all sorts of
musical misery. At one
point I was tempted to have
my son sing the rhythm for
Bobby to show him even a
five-year-old could at least

> **Despite my lack of encouragement, he had done what I thought was impossible.**

parrot the proper rhythm. Needless to say, Bobby did
not make all-region jazz or concert bands that year
either.

Same thing the next year. Another late evening
lesson, more tired feet and glassy eyes. I was secretly
hoping that he would not show up, but true to his

nature Bobby walked in right on time with his battered trumpet. But this night things were to be different. I am not sure what happened, but somehow Bobby had improved dramatically. While still no Wynton Marsalis, Bobby played in a way that gave a flicker of hope for his long-awaited chance at being an all-region player. It was kind of like the movie *Phenomenon* where John Travolta's character amazingly develops unbelievable mental capabilities, only on a much more modest scale. I almost asked him if he had been struck by lightning on the way to the bandroom. As the lesson progressed, I gained new energy with each properly played pitch, rhythm, and dynamic marking. His tone was actually pretty good considering his embouchure was still faulty.

The next week at all-region tryouts I nervously waited for the results, hoping that Bobby might just squeeze into the last position. His making it would help assuage my guilt at having given up on him years before. When the trumpet results were posted, I read down the list. Not until I got to the last qualifying position did I see Bobby's name. He had made it! Despite my lack of encouragement, he had done what I thought was impossible.

Bobby graduated several years ago, and he visits from time to time, always eager to know who is the latest recipient of the Bobby Jax "I've Fallen and I Can't Get Up Award". But during those months when he does not visit, Bobby lives on because he comes to mind each time I begin to dismiss a student as hopeless. God bless the Bobbys of this world. They may be the best teachers of all.

When I
Was a Kid . . .

The good old days. Things were so much harder when we were in band. Ironically, they were so much better as well. When in a particularly reflective mood, I relate these fond (or not so fond) memories to my students.

. . . our bandroom wasn't air-conditioned.

. . . we marched in three-mile parades that were uphill both ways.

. . . we did a different halftime show each week.

. . . we wore overlays on our uniforms, which were hotter than anyone today would believe possible.

. . . no boy had hair that hung over his uniform collar.

. . . we played more marches.

. . . we wore big hats that looked like oversized Q-tips®.

. . . we had more uniform parts than you could shake a stick at—from the plumes on our heads to the spats on our feet.

. . . we only had one bass drum in the marching band and couldn't even spell quad-tom.

. . . we played cornet from beginning band until we graduated.

. . . scores were often condensed and difficult to decipher at first glance.

. . . the only ensemble music was from Rubank books.

. . . our band director didn't earn what it costs to buy a sousaphone nowadays.

. . . drum majors twirled a mace and never gave a salute that looked like a Bruce Lee karate move.

. . . a big trip for our high school band was going to a thirty-mile away game, not Disney World.

. . . I never left my horn at school overnight.

. . . a tuner weighed about thirty pounds.

. . . a Yamaha was only something you rode on.

. . . we had cakewalks as fund-raisers.

. . . all band directors had to do drill design by hand.

...drum majors twirled a mace and never gave a salute that looked like a Bruce Lee karate move.

. . . sousaphones were so heavy they would give you a collapsed lung on your left side.

. . . we used reel-to-reel recorders.

. . . all trombone players had to reach out *all the way* to sixth and seventh positions. No triggers in those days.

. . . we played at games so cold that the mouthpieces stuck to the lips of our entire brass line and had to be surgically removed.

. . . only boys could be in band (if you can say this you go *way-y-y* back).

. . . the traditional drum grip was the *only* grip.

. . . they showed the bands at halftime on TV.

. . . our band only formed symmetrical pictures during halftime—none of this Picasso looking stuff.

. . . we only had three valves on our baritones.

. . . euphonium players didn't get so upset when someone called their instruments baritones.

. . . we stood at attention in 100 degree heat with the gnats so thick you could cut them with a baton.

. . . people came to the game just to see the band.

. . . we used a high-knee march that would ruin two pairs of pants a week during practice.

. . . jazz band was called stage band or lab band.

. . . we would march at halftime no matter how bad the weather conditions. I remember one rainy evening when the mud reached my register key.

. . . our band director wouldn't put up with any funny business. He could pierce a fly with his baton.

. . . we would copy all of our marching music (by hand, mind you) into a copy book. No copiers in those days.

. . . a Claude T. Smith 7/8 measure was about the only mixed meter we ever saw. No David Holsinger stuff in those days.

. . . Frederick Fennell's picture was on the inside cover of all our concert folders just like it is today.

. . . we played E-flat horn parts.

. . . we only played transcriptions.

. . . band directors wore uniforms too.

The Good News and the Bad News

No one can perfectly predict the future of band directing, but it will likely be a mixture of good and bad. The following are some of my predictions.

The Good News: Student-line alto saxophones will cost $5,000.

The Bad News: Each year fifty parents in your community will still find the money to buy them.

More Bad News: Your child will want to play one.

The Good News: Computers will be able to do amazing things in the field of music education.

The Bad News: Schools still won't be able to afford the technology.

More Bad News: IBM will develop an android named Mr. Holland that will take your job.

The Good News: Fund-raising candy will remain fifty cents to a dollar.

The Bad News: Boxes of M&M's will only have four M&Ms.

The Good News: Colleges and universities will add more relevant music education classes to their curriculums.

The Bad News: It will take seven years to earn a music education degree.

The Good News: Rap will no longer be popular.

The Bad News: Rap star Snoop Doggy Dog will make a comeback after sixty years in prison.

The Good News: *Mr. Holland's Opus* will become a
                  TV series.

The Bad News: It will star Arnold Schwarzenegger
                  as Mr. Holland and Madonna as
                  Rowena.

The Good News: Directors will continue to exert a
                  great influence over the lives of
                  their students.

The Bad News: Directors can be sued for smiling
                  at their students.

The Good News: Voice-activated drill design will be
                  invented by software companies.

The Bad News: Directors will still have to generate
                  creative ideas to make it work.

The Good News: Educational services will be
                  available in the home through the
                  use of advanced telecommuni-
                  cations.

The Bad News: Directors will teach band on closed-circuit television.

More Bad News: Students will graduate in two years.

The Good News: Woodwind players will use plastic reeds that sound as good as cane reeds and last forever.

The Bad News: When thrown across the room, these new reeds will leave permanent scars on unsuspecting victims.

The Good News: Air travel will be faster and less expensive than ever.

The Bad News: Band parents and students will not be satisfied with trips inside the contiguous United States.

The Good News: Bands will enjoy more visibility than ever.

The Bad News: Bands will march on professional wrestling productions.

The Good News: Companies will produce music stands that are indestructible.

The Bad News: The material they use causes cancer in laboratory animals.

The Good News: More administrators will be former band directors.

The Bad News: More administrators will be former band directors.

The Good News: Band uniforms will have fewer parts.

The Bad News: They will cost $1,000 each.

The Good News: Cable television will introduce The Band Channel.

The Bad News: Local critics will review band concerts.

The Good News: Schools will furnish safer school buses for band trips.

The Bad News: All passengers will be required to wear helmets.

The Good News: Band director salaries will rise.

The Bad News: Minimum wage will go even higher.

Just Chill

As contest season approaches, I try to follow what might seem like unusual advice—just chill. My students use this short phrase quite regularly when they see someone getting way too uptight, taking something way too seriously.

I am reminded of our school's ROTC sergeant, a fine teacher and otherwise nice guy who rhetorically asks everyone at each faculty meeting if he is the only one enforcing the rules. One year my band was going to perform PDQ Bach's wacky *Grand Serenade for an Awful Lot of Winds and Percussion* at an evening performance. To add comedic effect to the ending, we asked a band student's dad, who moonlighted as a country clown named Uncle Dan, to do his country hick act on the final movement while serving as our cymbal player. To help publicize the concert, he visited the school during lunch hour and mingled with students while outfitted in his overalls, blackened teeth, and straw hat. While eating lunch, our zealous sergeant, observing a serious breach of school policy, approached Uncle Dan and asked him to remove his hat. In response to the sergeant's request, Uncle Dan did what any self-respecting clown would do—he slowly removed the straw hat only to plop it down on his head again while plastering a stupid grin across his face. Infuriated by this brash breach of military protocol, Sarge flushed as he repeated his order.

> **Our zealous sergeant, observing a serious breach of school policy, approached Uncle Dan and asked him to remove his hat.**

And, as you might expect, Uncle Dan repeated his theatrics for his adoring teenage audience. Without a school court-martial as an option, Sarge marched into the faculty dining area and mercilessly lambasted the "sorry Bozo" (an interesting choice of words) for his insubordination.

It was at that point I informed him that the man in question was a band parent dressed in costume. To which this man of Northern heritage tartly replied, "How was I supposed to know? Half the people in Arkansas dress that way!"

Without commenting on the accuracy of his remark, let me say that what Sarge needed to do was "just chill".

Sometimes we take ourselves too seriously. I suppose the one accusation kids love to level at us more than any other is "You think band is all there is in life." While I will sometimes kiddingly respond to such a remark with "What else is there?" I take the comment rather personally since I try to have a rather balanced life myself. However, I find it important to constantly reassess the delicate balance between my zealous attempt at musical success and the various commitment levels of band students who enroll in music for a myriad of reasons.

Successful music making requires intensity and concentration, but not to the point that it stifles students who, if we are not careful, may become musical pawns in our drive toward success and adoration from our peers and the music world in general.

Find creative ways to lighten up, despite the pressures surrounding you. During marching rehearsals my band takes a five-minute vacation: members lie down right where they are on the field, close their eyes, and take five-minute mental vacations to anywhere in the world they want to go. (With our hot Arkansas summers, Alaska and Canada are popular places!) During concert season, we take a moment in the middle of class to enjoy a joke-of-the-day or sing "Happy Birthday" to students who have birthdays that week. Simple things like these can serve to re-energize sagging rehearsals just by the positive feelings they promote.

Most of all, maintain a sense of humor during the weeks leading up to important performances. Seize unexpected light moments as chances to give rehearsals a gentle ebb and flow of intensity. Our goal as teachers and mentors should be to create a rewarding and exciting journey rather than merely focusing all energies on reaching the final destination.

As contests draw near, study those scores, rehearse with vigor and intensity, and if things get too stressful, remember . . . *just chill.*

Speech 101

I am turning into my high school band director. The signs were barely noticeable at first—a little hair loss, tighter fitting slacks, a little ribbing from my students about my age and choice of clothes. The metamorphosis became undeniable when I began giving speeches to students at the slightest of provocations. I even found myself repeating many of the speeches I heard as a student.

At a rational level I know I shouldn't feel too bad about this. It is a time-honored tradition for band directors to give advice and tell stories that we hope will terrify students into doing what's right. Although older students may occasionally scoff at these stories, most beginners will listen with rapt attention to our tidbits of wisdom and experience.

Beginning band students are more likely to maintain their instruments properly if told the right story. I stress the importance of cleaning the inner slides of trombones with a story that a repair technician told me several years ago. A student brought him a trombone that would not produce a sound and caused a backlog of air each time he blew into the instrument. Upon further inspection, the technician found three mice (whether they were blind or not I couldn't say) clogged in the bottom of the slide. The message here: *Clean the inside of your instruments regularly and keep your cases closed at night.*

Funky Winkerbean cartoon reprinted with special permission of North America Syndicate.

To prevent woodwind players from leaving their reeds on the mouthpieces after playing, one director I know tells them about a former student who left his reed on the mouthpiece so long that not only did the reed stay on the mouthpiece without need of a ligature but turned a rainbow of disgusting colors resulting from month-old food particles. The student checked out of school one day and never came back. (I believe the last part is a slight embellishment.) The point here: *Remove the reed after each playing session and clean the mouthpiece regularly to avoid catching some dreaded disease!*

> **The student checked out of school one day and never came back.**

I also tell students not to touch equipment that does not belong to them. One year several of my students, without permission, attempted to move an old decrepit piano that was tucked away in the corner of the bandroom. It fell on one kid and broke his pelvis in eighteen places. Amazingly enough, he recovered fully, but the message is clear: *Don't touch equipment in this room that does not belong to you. It might unexpectedly break in your hands or flatten you like a pancake!*

Although high school kids are harder to impress with stories, some can be effective. In marching band, I tell stories of band members who locked their knees while standing at attention in the heat of summer and fell over, straight as a board. One year we had a trombone player and future drum major who lasted all of five minutes at his first summer rehearsal before he locked his knees and keeled over like a sheet of plywood. So now we tell them: *Don't lock your knees or you might fall on your face. Make it at least five minutes and you won't break the shortest endurance record.*

Kids also love to pull chairs out from other students, a practice I discourage by telling the tale of a violent incident at the junior high school. A saxophone player was about to sit when someone pulled the chair out from under him. The mouthpiece and reed jammed into his chin when he hit the ground and the cut required four stitches. After relating this story I emphasize that they should *never pull a chair out from under another student. You could severely injure someone and have the incident put on your PERMANENT RECORD.*

Unfortunately, I think I now have a speech for just about every situation a band student could find himself in. (I think kids behave better now just so they don't have to listen to me anymore.) Maybe it's not too late to turn back time a little and stop the gradual transformation into my high school band director. A little Rogaine, a Slim-Fast diet, Grecian formula, and a new wardrobe might do the trick. I can always stop telling so many stories. Others have done it. In fact, I knew this band director who....

Mrs. Whittle

She was mean. At least ten feet tall and as tough as beef jerky, Mrs. Whittle was pure, unadulterated mean. It was rumored that she lived in a candy house and ate kids for supper. She must have taught fifth grade science forever, and when Mrs. Whittle discussed the Cenozoic Era you believed whatever she said because you knew she had been there when it happened.

She had several levels of meanness. The slightest of infractions would bring a finger-wagging tirade that would make Mike Tyson run for cover. For infractions she deemed more serious, she would grab your hand, turn it over to the underside of your wrist, and begin whacking your wrist with the backside of her index and middle fingers. Her verbal assault was a perfectly

121

timed duet with each stroke—"IF-I'VE-TOLD-YOU-ONCE-I'VE-TOLD-YOU-A-MILLION-TIMES-**NOT**-TO DO-THAT!"

For the most heinous of infractions, she would get right in your face, providing a much closer view of her facial features than you would otherwise have preferred. Once eye contact was established she would dramatically orate a sentence honed to perfection with countless practice—**"HOW RUDE OF YOU!"** With more skill than a Shakespearean actress, she would manipulate the words, squeezing every inch of meaning from them like a farmer milking the last squirt from a cow. The word **HOW** began breathy and soft like a dog's growl and grew slowly until the **D** in **RUDE** clacked against her teeth with a violent "duh" that rang for what seemed like an eternity. After the appropriate time elapsed for dramatic effect, she would conclude with a relatively short **OF** that would quickly crescendo into the climactic **YOU-U-U-U-U-U-U** that would fade away into nothingness, leaving little in its wake but a terrified kid whose sympathetic friends were snickering furiously as they covered their mouths with their hands.

As if this wasn't enough, the sixth graders told us that she would get very mad at the end of the year and might even cry. With only two days of school left,

Mt. Vesuvius erupted. It all began when a friend of mine broke his pencil lead and asked Mrs. Whittle if he could sharpen it. With a snappy "NO!" Mrs. Whittle stomped out of the room. Being the helpful friend that I am, I took the pencil to sharpen it for

> **As she said the word "crucifies," her hands flew out as if she had indeed been nailed to a cross.**

him while she was gone. Just as I was about halfway across the room, Mrs. Whittle returned. I froze from fear, uncertain of what to do next. As she slowly began pacing back and forth, I hunkered down and eased back to my seat. Fortunately for me she began to address the whole class, not just me. She began pacing faster and faster, her face growing redder with each crisply performed about-face. Her breathing grew heavier and louder. So loud in fact, I thought steam was going to come of out her ears at any second. Her agitated movements culminated with a climactic burst of agony as she screamed, "It just *crucifies* me how you treat me!" As she said the word "crucifies" her hands flew out as if she had indeed been nailed to a cross. After this shocking introduction, she began to recite all the good things she had done for us. She even asked for our opinions once during the tirade: "If you think I do a good job, raise your hand." As we sat there motionless, too stunned to move, she yelled, "GET YOUR HANDS UP!!!!!" We hastily complied.

She may have been mean, but Mrs. Whittle was a good teacher. She had the most colorful room in the school. When the school year began, her room had a wintry bleakness that burst into spring as our science projects filled the room after weeks of drawing, cutting, pasting, and painting. Handcrafted projects lined the shelves, drawings were pinned to bulletin boards, and mobiles hung from the ceiling.

Mrs. Whittle kept us making things and *learning*. And what's more, she never said anything disparaging about what we made. Take my Saturn project, for instance. My assignment was to construct a Saturn to hang from the ceiling with the other eight planets. As I was prone to do, I didn't tell my mother about the project until the last minute and worse yet, I could remember very little of how Mrs. Whittle said to make it. I did remember that we needed a balloon, glue, and strips of newspaper but that was it.

Frustrated by my ambiguous directions, my mother purchased some papier mâché gook that looked like oatmeal. We applied what seemed like ten pounds of the stuff to a balloon only to see large canyons form as the gook dried. At this point we decided to apply strips of newspaper covered with glue on top of the gook. This worked, but by the time we finished, the second largest planet moved into first place. When we added the rings it

Mrs. Whittle didn't make one discouraging remark about my obese planet.

became even larger. It didn't help matters that the bright orange color we used to paint the planet was absorbed by the newspaper and gook, forming a light, sickening orange color, sure to blend wonderfully with the gaggy green paint on the school walls (improves the learning environment they said at the time).

With some embarrassment, I carried my Saturn to class the next morning. Mrs. Whittle didn't make one discouraging remark about my obese planet. She looked pleased as she took great care in hanging it next to Jupiter. It didn't matter that it dwarfed the galaxy's largest planet, making it appear as a mere moon.

Despite her personal faults, there was no mistaking it—Mrs. Whittle wanted us to learn science. At the time I thought she hated kids, but I have since come to the conclusion that if she really hated us she

wouldn't have tried so hard to make us learn. I realize
now that Mrs. Whittle represents one end of a
challenge we all face—balancing our own need to be
liked with student learning. She chose, consciously or
not, to put student learning over her own popularity.
Some might say she loved science and hated kids, but I
disagree. If she hated kids she wouldn't have tried so
passionately to teach them.

The issue of teacher popularity versus student
learning may seem irrelevant but let's face it, most
teachers want to be liked and our teaching is, in fact,
influenced by our conscious or subconscious need to be
liked and appreciated. Inexperienced teachers are often
lax in discipline because they want to be liked. During
my first year of teaching, I was particularly conscious
of how well-liked I was by students because I wanted
so badly to have a positive impact on their lives. I soon
found that this need to be popular was at odds with
many of the goals I had set for my band program. I
found that students who were not willing to meet my
high expectations did not take a particular liking to me.
I also was not popular with students who thought I
should do things the way they had always been done
in the past nor with students who would not behave.

I certainly believe that students will work
harder and learn more if they like me, but when

conflicts arise, do I lower goals and expectations because the kids don't like them and don't like me? I followed six years of directing at the junior high level with two difficult years at the high school level. I inherited a high school band that was not used to doing what it takes to be successful. I had taught many of the students in junior high school where we accomplished some great things, but many of them were not willing to raise their commitment level high enough to be a great high school band. The poor attitudes and lack of close-knit unity really hurt me personally, but I believed that developing excellence in music was more important than what they thought of me. I did a lot of soul-searching, and although I certainly made mistakes, I knew that I was treating the students in a fair and caring manner. After my second year at the high school level, junior high students entered the senior program with high expectations firmly established, and they had little problem accepting them.

I can think of many teachers that I liked personally, but I learned very little in their classes. They were popular with students, but for the wrong reasons. I can think of others I did not particularly like but imparted a great deal about their subject areas. Such teachers have been harshly criticized by those who emphasize student feelings and self-esteem, but we should not forget that amidst this wave of "feel-good" philosophy, we must keep our expectations high and pass on a passion for music and learning. If we don't, the Mrs. Whittles of the world will find us very rude indeed.

Marching
Through Wal-Mart

I remember the pride I felt wearing my high school band uniform for the first time. I was also a little nervous because I had to undergo my first uniform inspection by the band council. It wasn't easy making sure that all the doo-dads, overlays, spats, and assorted gizmos were attached correctly. I passed inspection but was a little embarrassed when I was told that the plume on the band hat was backward. After correcting the problem, I was even more embarrassed to find that it didn't matter which way the plume was put in, it still looked the same. I was the victim of *tradition*. In fact, I perpetuated the practice the next year on other unsuspecting sophomores because it was . . . well . . . tradition.

Whenever I hear the word "tradition," there seems to be a certain musicality to it. I envision Tevye, the father in *Fiddler on the Roof*, bursting into song with his arms outstretched while dancing to the music. While tradition is often acknowledged from a general standpoint as in the overall excellence of a band program, directors should be quick to recognize and encourage much smaller traditions as well. The seemingly small and insignificant traditions serve as glue to hold groups together and provide some of the fondest memories for band members.

Marching band lends itself to many traditions, starting as early as summer practices. Every summer we begin what we call our adopt-a-rookie program. Upperclassmen adopt new senior high band members (rookies) and are responsible for making sure that these kids know the ropes. Our goal is to encourage the new students to be an integral part of the band. The upperclassmen are responsible for making sure the rookies have a ride to and from rehearsal. We have some that live a good distance from the school and cannot be in band if they do not have help with transportation. The upperclassmen are also responsible for making sure their rookies know the rookie poem (sung to the tune of "The Beverly Hillbillies") and are prepared to perform a skit on the last day of summer practice. After the skits, upperclassmen treat the rookies to pizza at a local restaurant to reward them for their hard work.

> . . .seemingly small traditions serve as glue to hold groups together and provide some of the fondest memories . . .

After one of our summer practices, we have our now-traditional kickball game. The assistant director and I team up with the freshmen and seniors to take on the sophomores and juniors. The opposing players really enjoy throwing us out every now and then; they get an extra thrill if they beat us. I have to admit I do feel a little younger when my team wins and I am lucky enough to make a good play of some type.

At the conclusion of summer practices, we have a cookout and performance for the parents. The color guard performs a routine they learned at camp, the percussion plays a cadence, and then the full band takes the field. Before we perform, we show the parents how we teach drill and demonstrate some of the moves we will use in our first show. After the band plays, we teach some of the parents basic commands and have them compete in a "drill down" where the drum major gives commands and the last parent to make a mistake wins. Then we have the students perform the drill down. The students exhibit a lot of pride in showing their parents how it's done. Then we all enjoy a cookout prepared by the band boosters.

It's also a tradition to have the seniors and band council members over to my house each fall the week before our first game. The kids enjoy this since it is probably the only time they have actually been in a teacher's house. We visit, eat, and then have a meeting to discuss goals for the year.

Some traditions center around the music that is played at football games. We play "Hey Baby!" at the beginning of every game as a sort of welcome to the other band. I didn't play it at an away game once and my kids almost revolted so we played it at the end of the game. Fortunately, we won the game so it fit the mood of the crowd. I hadn't fully realized until that night that playing "Hey Baby!" at the start of the game had evolved into a tradition.

Each year we have a "lock-in" where the kids stay up all night in the bandroom playing games, listening to music, eating, etc. We give out funny awards to recognize students for the inevitable funny situations that occur over the course of a year. I make sure every student receives some type of award. We also recognize everyone on our yearly "Ram Band News", a video of newsworthy band events that we record with the help of our school video department.

While many traditions result from conscious effort and implementation, some start quite unexpectedly. One of my band's traditions is marching through Wal-Mart. It started on a small scale one year when, on a whim, an upperclassman told a rookie to march up and down a couple of aisles at Wal-Mart. These caught on a little more each year until now all the rookies are gathered together during one of our summer lunch breaks and are paraded through Wal-Mart chanting "Always Saves" and other Wal-Mart slogans. The management at Wal-Mart has always been kind enough to give us permission to do this, and the regular shoppers really enjoy the show.

It's very important to recognize traditions when going into a new position. It is important to build your own program, but categorically ignoring traditions that were in place long before you arrived could erode support for your program. There are a number of traditions in our band now that have obscure origins, but they continue. On the Friday of homecoming week, we march through the halls of the school and stop periodically to play our stands tunes. We also play in the cafeteria for those eating lunch, and our final destination is the courtyard area where we jam until the homecoming assembly begins. Since our junior high is on the same campus, we march through the junior high as well. This gives us a chance for a little publicity with the junior high students. It's awfully loud, but fun.

Another long-time tradition of unknown origin is to "go get a pine cone". The outskirts of our practice field is surrounded by pine trees so students with slight infractions during marching season are told to run and find a pine cone in the band of trees. One year I ran and got one because I let them out of a rehearsal late when I said I wouldn't.

One warning about traditions. Like Tevye in *Fiddler on the Roof*, we must let go of some traditions when they lose their effectiveness. When I was in high school our band did the same entrance, marched to our fight song, for two straight years and while that might work for some, our band members did not like it and the director was very slow to respond. It wasn't until a faction of our student body booed and we were thoroughly embarrassed that things were changed. Directors should make sure traditions aren't theirs and theirs alone.

It is important to recognize the significance of traditions and build your program around them. Traditions, large and small, often become the fondest memories for students many years later. They also serve as a tie between band members of old and later generations. My oldest child is going to be in band soon, and you can bet I'll make sure she has her plume in correctly.

Inspired
Instrument Maintenance

Anyone can play an instrument that works, but those who produce music with stuck tuning slides and permanently impacted clarinet swabs are the prodigies of our bands. I suppose that if a typical band student wrote an article on instrument maintenance it would probably be like the following.

Trumpet players should insert the mouthpiece in the leadpipe and bring a hand down sharply on it to lodge it firmly and permanently in the instrument. This avoids the problem of dropping it during a concert or losing it between rehearsals. The added length can be accommodated by simply buying a larger case.

The little rod that comes with each flute can be used to clean the instrument, but it is better suited for poking clarinet players when the director is not looking. Never clean flute tenons; any difficulties in adding or removing a foot joint will build character and wrist muscles.

Horn players should not waste time greasing all of those slides when they can get by lubricating only the main slides on the double horn. Unless your band director was a horn major, you will never need the others.

Clarinet players should only swab their instruments in two instances. Always swab before a clinic by a professional clarinet player if you like your director and want him to look good, or, as a test of strength, try pulling the swab up from the bell to see if you can dislodge it from the clarinet's narrow end. If you can't do it, have a contest to see who is the strongest in the band.

Trombone players should display their unique personalities by tripping unsuspecting friends with their slide as they pass by. Any resulting dents in the slides will strengthen biceps and make Fillmore marches more challenging.

Saxophone players should leave the reed on the mouthpiece when not in use. After several months, you can challenge other sax players to discover whose reed stays on the mouthpiece the longest when the ligature is removed. Losing your neck-strap is nothing to worry about; most students find they can play satisfactorily by omitting all C#'s and any key requiring it or its enharmonic D♭.

The euphonium and tuba serve nicely as storage areas for old music, love notes, and past homework assignments, so feel free to stuff these items into the bell. If the tone becomes muffled, simply blow a little harder. Besides, muted euphonium and tuba parts are often called for in junior high literature.

Double reed players will want to eat something gummy before practicing. Tootsie Rolls, Sugar Babies, bubble gum, and caramels form an effective amalgam on the inside of key holes so that when raising a key the effect will be something like bubble gum on the bottom of a shoe. The instrument will produce gratifying contemporary music sounds as the pads ooze up from the keyholes. Reeds used for extended periods will develop interesting colors and flavors, but before exchanging reeds with others in your section, be sure to wipe the germs off with your shirtsleeve.

Percussionists need not replace the wire snares until the last one breaks because farsighted manufacturers constructed the instrument with spare ones built in. Never return auxiliary percussion instruments to the storage cabinet; it is the director's job, usually specified in his contract, to crawl under chairs and around stands to retrieve tambourines, triangle beaters, and suspended cymbal mallets.

Any time you leave your seat during rehearsal, balance your instrument on a sturdy folding chair under the close supervision of fellow band members. Avoid the rush in leaving the rehearsal room by putting your instrument away several measures before the end of the session; verify that all latches are solidly closed by dropping the instrument and case from a height of at least two feet.

If these suggestions do not maintain your instrument's prime condition, have it examined by your parents or a pawnshop. There is no use bothering your band director until the day of the concert.

Memories
of a Lifetime

Whenever directors question whether music programs really make a difference, a note of thanks from a student, a kind word from a parent, or a hug at graduation can dispel all doubts. Some directors may even receive a letter from a former student, who after many years realizes the need to express how much the director or an ensemble influenced his life. One of those affirmations of our influence came to me in quite an unexpected way.

Several years ago I returned from a trip to discover that Ed Raines, a fifty-five-year-old member of our church, had died suddenly. Although I did not know him well, I met his son Denny at church and saw him frequently at school. While visiting the family at the funeral home, I was pleasantly surprised to see that there was an easel set up in the funeral parlor with several photos of Ed during his days as a member of the Paragould High School band in the late 1950s and early 1960s. One photo showed him practicing his baritone, another sweating heavily after a grueling marching band practice where as drum major he was running the band through their paces, another leading the band in a parade, and one at a lighter moment where he was hanging out with some of the majorettes.

It immediately struck me that the family had selected photographs from his high school days as drum major rather than more recent photos. While talking to Lanay, Ed's wife, I discovered that the family had chosen to display the band pictures because they knew many former band members would be attending and might like to see them. She also said that Ed always felt that band and track were the two things that "saved" him. His father was an alcoholic and band served as his refuge from difficulties at home and gave him great confidence and pride. Ed's mother, Verda, told me that one of her proudest moments was at the Paragould Christmas parade when Ed strutted right over to where she was standing in the crowd and deeply bowed to her before zigzagging back to the band. She said that Ed always appreciated the fact that his director John Cooper believed in him even at times

Ed Raines – photo compliments of family

when he felt like no one else did. Although Ed did not make music his life's work, he did become a teacher and taught band briefly along with his normal teaching duties for a short time.

Over the subsequent weeks I reflected on how band directors really have the power to make memories of a lifetime. No matter what our students do after graduation, they will always remember their experiences in band with joy, indifference, or regret. What will they remember? Ratings? The trips? A kind word? An insult? Friendships? Leadership roles? Individual awards? Performances? Although many memories are forged without our help, there is no doubt that we affect each aspect of their memories to some degree, particularly their concepts of what they contributed to the band.

> . . . we become so wrapped up in the problems of the moment . . . we lose our perspective and forget to see band members as individuals.

My most inspiring early influence was Cathy Patrick, my junior high band director in Auburn, Alabama. Many years and relocations have caused us to lose contact but memories remain. I remember getting a progress report usually reserved for those struggling with their grades. Somewhat concerned, I looked at the form and was relieved to see that Miss Patrick was telling my parents how well I was doing. In senior high (in another city) I worked very hard, waiting for compliments that never came. I now send a personal handwritten note to every student at least once before they graduate. I try to focus on complimenting individuals, not just the group as a whole.

In the afterword to the book *Good-Bye Mr. Chips,* author James Hilton observes that "no two schools are alike, but more than that—a school with two hundred pupils is really two hundred schools, and among them, almost certainly, are somebody's long-remembered heaven and somebody else's hell." Likewise, I suggest that a band with two hundred members is actually two hundred bands, each with different needs and different perspectives. Sometimes we become so wrapped up in the problems of the moment, performances, ratings, and the pressure to accomplish so much in so little time that we lose our perspective and forget to see the band members as individuals. Our task, however daunting, is to remember that each student is an individual, making memories that will last a lifetime.

Epilogue

"You are going to be the death of me yet." This sentiment, like many others uttered by my parents and teachers during childhood, has taken on true meaning during my teaching career. More than once I have kiddingly told my band that if I were blessed to live long enough to conduct a band during my twilight years, it would probably be a missed key signature, a misplayed rhythm, or an unexpected exposure to "Louie Louie" that would stop the old ticker for good.

Actually, visions of my demise are somewhat more hopeful. I would like nothing better than to keel over after conducting the ultimate performance of Holst's *First Suite in E♭*. Except for the fact that it would be somewhat of a downer for the audience (not to mention extra work for the custodian after the concert), this would be a great way to go.

Unfortunately, it is a rare moment when individuals can script their own coda; few will end it all in a blaze of glory like Michael Jordan nailing the last shot of his career to win an NBA Championship. Most will go rather quietly with no special visits from the governor at a farewell school assembly like in the movie *Mr. Holland's Opus*.

But quietly does not mean unproductively. While aging athletes are confined to watching videotapes and highlight clips of performances never to be repeated or improved, musicians can improve to the very end—performances of pianists Arthur Rubenstein and Vladimer Horowitz testify to that fact.

I am inspired when I remember seeing the famous brass pedagogue Arnold Jacobs at the Mid-West clinic a couple of years before his death. A crowd had gathered to watch the venerable, octogenarian tubist try out a new model at an exhibit. What began as a simple desire to try out a new tuba became a moment of wonder as convention attendees stopped to marvel at a master at work.

Indeed, musicians are staying active and doing great things well past what used to seem possible. About ten years ago, I saw Maynard Ferguson perform with a new band he had just formed. He was the only musician in the band over the age of twenty-four. Even today, when he must be at least one hundred and thirty years old, Ferguson is still swingin' as hard as ever.

God bless you in whatever future your career in music brings. Work hard, have fun, and like Maynard, go down swingin'!

Appendix

One Christmas I was browsing in my favorite bookstore when I noticed a small, old book that contained humorous poems about various members of the orchestra. I thought it was a neat idea and decided to try my hand at it. I'm not sure how I decided on the limerick as my standard poetical device other than the fact that as a kid I enjoyed the nonsensical verse of Edward Lear, "the father of English nonsense". Also, limericks are easier to write than Japanese haiku.

I added these poems as an appendix for two reasons. First, there's nothing like an appendix to make a book appear more sophisticated. Secondly, I thought it would be fun to offer everyone the opportunity to participate in a brief "Look, I'm a surgeon!" fantasy: if you don't like the poems, you can remove the appendix since it really isn't necessary. (Sorry, I just couldn't resist.)

There once was a man who played trumpet
While eating his tea and his crumpets.
His wife said it rude to play with his food,
But he said to "like it or lump it!"

There once was a boy from Aruba
Who aspired to play on the tuba.
He blew it so loud it could be heard from a cloud,
So his parents Fed-Exed it to Cuba.

There once was a man
who was Russian
Who loved to beat on
percussion.
He struck with such
force that his stick lost its
course
And gave him a major
concussion!

There once was a sickly old fellow
Who expired in Act I of *Othello*.
   Informed that he died,
    the conductor replied,
      "How could I know?
       He played cello!"

There once was a silver euphonium
All alone in its case—how Draconian!
Then a beginner was switched and the latches
unhitched,
And now it wreaks pure pandemonium!

There once was a Greek named Medusa
Who danced to the marches of Sousa.
With the strains so divine the snakes would keep time
In a way that would downright amuse ya!

There once were some army platoons
That marched and played on bassoons.
Without breaking their reeds,
they accomplished great deeds
As their foes ran to hide from their tunes!

There once was a man from Monsoon
Who played on a contrabassoon.
The conductor would moan that the sound of his tone
Was like that of a leaking balloon.

There once was a maestro from Firth,
Whose ego kept growing from birth.
Then one day he tried
to swallow his pride
And added five pounds to his girth!

There once was a marching instructor
Who let no bad weather obstruct her.
Though lightning was near, she never showed fear
For she was a sorry conductor!

Suggested Reading

*Musicians should spend as much time as possible adding to their knowledge. To aid in this endeavor, many books have helpful lists of suggested reading at the end of them. This is **not** one of those. Don't try finding any of these anywhere because you won't.*

Books

History of the Mass by Agnes Dei with a foreword by Kerry A. Elasone.

Cutting and Scraping Techniques for Woodwinds by Chip Reed.

The Marches of Franz Schubert by Marge Militaire.

Making it to the Top with Music by D.C. "Al" Coda.

Let Me Be Me by Gedoffemi Bach.

Improve Your Conducting by Claire Ictus.

Tuning Techniques for Brasses by Ben Sharp and Will Flatt.

Playing the Oboe in Tune by Cantby Dunne.

Performance Problems by Discant B. Wright, Mister Cue, and Tim Poe Dragon.

Earning Money with Music by Macon Lute and Jullien Dollars.

Making Money Playing Horn by Ken Ivan Crook.

Early German Vocalists by Minnie Singer.

Pavarotti—Future Talk Show Host by Opera Winfrey.

Form in Music by Ron Doe.

The History of Dance by Sarah Band.

César—An Unauthorized Biography by Vera Franck.

Rehearsal Preparation by Louis Gottschalk.

Hemiola in Modern Music by Polly Rhythm.

Performance Anxiety by Hugo Furst.

A Band Director's Guide to Washington, D.C. by Seymour Lyres.

Where Are They Now? A Look at Composers in Seclusion by I. Ben Haydn.

Symphonic Music Used in Cartoons by Donald Tweedy and William Byrd.

Periodicals

"Influences of al Fresco Art on Bald Renaissance Composers" by Girolamo Frescobaldi.

"Italian Eating Habits and the Diet of Giuseppe Verdi" by Aida Lott and M.T. Buffet.

"The Spanish Dances of Ravel" by Bo Larro.

"The Unperformed Operas of Moussorgsky" by Arnotte Godunov, Eura Bohr, Will Jahn, and "Sleepy" Mendoza.

"Speech Problems and Their Effects on Brass Players" by Tom Bone.

"Influence of Renaissance Madrigals on Spanish Composers" by Manuel De Fa-la-la-la-la.

"Flem-Flams: How the Flemish School Influenced Modern Drumming" by Perry Diddle.

"The Useless Rudiment" by Segno T. Drags.

"Great Christmas Presents for Music Lovers" by Carol Liszt and Yule B. Chopin.

"Instrument Care and Beginning Band Students" by Juan Mordent.

"Allusions to Fish in Handel's Water Music" by Ima Sourdine, Melody Scales, and Eaton Hooks.

"The Last Days of Mozart" by Di Baroque, Ode Cash, and Barry M. Nicholas.

"Horn Parts in Gruesome Country Square Dances of Nineteenth-Century America" by Corno Macabre.

"Music in Our Nation's Prisons" by Quattro Purcell.

"Embouchure Problems and How to Fix Them" by Cliff Lipps.

"Russian Violinists Who Also Played Percussion" by Efrem Cymbalist.

"Drinking Problems of Stephen Foster" by Phillip Glass, Henry Fillmore, Seconda Martini, and William Still.

"Percussionists—Do They Deserve their Reputation?" by Morceau Van Knot. With a rebuttal by R.U. Caesura.

"Hair Styles of Modern Composers" by Samuel Barber.

"Conducting, Gangrene and the Death of Jean-Baptiste Lully" by Cain Hertz Foote.

"Humility and Trumpet Players: A Historical Perspective" by C. Nunn Shofar.

"Jamaican Influences on American Music: A Symposium" with contributions by Goodman, Schumann, Hartmann, and Grossman.

"Childhood Ailments of Famous Jazz Musicians" by Gene Krupa.

"Famous Vegetarian Conductors" by Zubin Tom Mehta and Charles Munch.

"A Symposium on Carnival of the Animals " by Siegfried Ochs, Timothy Swan, Max Kowalski, Charles Horsley, and Thomas Oliphant.

"Composing for Video Games" by Vladimir de Pachmann.

"Fast Food and Its Effect on Performance" by Johann Taco Bell.

Glossary

Most glossaries are filled with terms used previously in that particular book. This one is not. I thought I would identify some things in the band world that needed to be recognized, named, and defined—a sort of "bandspeak."

aerotone-- n. sound a brass instrument makes when a cork is missing from the water key.

altissigreedy-- v. in trumpet players, the tendency to take high notes even higher and cracking them.

ambimaldexterous-- n. in woodwinds, the ability to miss the key signature with either hand.

anachropicture-- n. old, out-of-date photos (usually at least thirty years old) which composers and conductors use with their program notes, articles, or compositions. Also, dated photographs of people demonstrating proper posture and playing positions in band method books.

anthological wannebees-- n. dusty past issues of *The Instrumentalist* which accumulate on bandroom bookshelves.

antibanner-- v. to incorrectly twirl a flag in the opposite direction of the rest of the color guard.

aquasadist-- n. one who loves to let saliva ooze out of the water key while onlookers gross out.

batonize-- v. to throw a baton in such a way that it sticks in a tile ceiling.

bocal minority-- n. bassoonists.

bonelabel-- n. the round thing near the tuning slide of the trombone which usually bears the brand name of the trombone.

belldribble-- n. saliva which makes its way all the way through the instrument and exits through the bell.

bipodal-- n. a timpani missing one of its wheels.

caneshock-- n. the condition of
facial redness which occurs
when woodwind players use
a reed too strong for their
embouchures.

catalogjam-- n.
what happens
when no more
music catalogs can
be stuffed into your desk drawer.

chopedit-- v. to accidentally slice a portion of the
marching music when using the paper cutter.

chuckletone-- n. sound produced when a player
laughs and plays a note at the same time.

clattle-- v. to produce a clacking sound by loosening
valve caps and depressing and releasing the valves in a
rapid manner.

corkettes-- n. the little corks stuck between the keys of
new woodwind instruments.

cramdit-- v. to accidentally cram a mouthpiece into the leadpipe, thus requiring the use of a Thompson mouthpiece puller.

demochoir-- n. the anonymous group of singers who sing the vocal parts on all marching music.

denthead-- n. plastic keyboard mallet with several small sections of the head missing.

dentu-dents-- n. small teeth marks on a woodwind mouthpiece.

dinkleannies-- n. leftover band shoes of different styles in bandroom storage rooms, none of which has a matching partner.

drill dementia-- n. the sudden state of apathy and depression which occurs about halfway (sometimes much sooner) through the drill-writing process.

drumquake-- n. the violent shaking of the bandroom when a full marching percussion section plays fortissimo on a cadence.

ebonogrime-- n. the black, grimy substance which collects on the tenons of a flute.

emboucircle-- n. ring left on the lips after playing a brass instrument.

fiffle-- n. feathery-like substance which floats in the air when it comes free of a plume.

fixophobia-- n. the fear of repairing instruments.

flophorn-- n. old, decrepit brass instrument owned by the school for at least two hundred years.

foliomugged-- v. during marching season, to do a snappy horns up only to have the flip folder fly off the lyre and strike one in the head.

forple-- v. to make a sweeping motion with the hand and accidentally knock all the music off the music stand, usually to be shortly followed by laughter and applause.

framing-- v. making some obvious musical mistake and looking at the person next to you like *he* did it.

fundebris-- n. leftover fund-raising items.

gilbeed-- v.   on band trips, to be accidentally left behind in an eating establishment while the bus heads home.

groggling-- v. making a disgusting sound on a brass instrument by continuing to play when the water key should be emptied, but isn't.

groovlets-- n. the individual grooves on a cymbal.

gwabs-- n. wads of chewing gum stuck underneath band chairs.

harmonic retrograde-- n. when a poor flute player tries to play a two octave scale, but the second octave keeps dropping back to the first octave on each attempt.

heismaneuver-- v. putting out the left hand (a la Heisman trophy) to obtain a softer dynamic from the band.

hurping-- v. hiccuping while trying to play an instrument.

hydraprayer-- n. a request made to the heavens for rain when the halftime show isn't ready.

igniquery-- n. a dumb question asked by a student who would have known the answer if he had been listening thirty seconds before asking the question.

inebristand-- n. a wobbly music stand.

instructonesia-- n. the condition whereby one gets the band's attention only to promptly forget what you are going to say.

jinglets-- n. small, metal rings on a tambourine.

leadslurm-- n. collection of food bits in leadpipe.

machoerr-- v. an attempt to display strength and "macho" by extracting a mouthpiece by hand and then accidentally ruining the leadpipe and unsoldering various connections.

minifib-- v. when a band director tells the band "One more time."

McMania-- n. two hundred students in a fast food restaurant.

morphan-- n. a percussion mallet with no matching partner.

moolahmoocher-- n. a student who never participates in a band fund-raiser.

muchopapyri-- n. sheets of paper (old homework assignments, love notes, music which should have been turned in, etc.) found in instrument cases.

muffitti-- n. the writing on music stands (love lives, tic-tac-toe, etc.).

mustonium-- n. initial blast of odor upon opening an old instrument case.

mutations-- n. dents in a metal mute.

neonote trauma-- n. when sight-reading, the body's reaction to being totally lost.

nocturnal grids-- n. during marching season, the drill paper designs which appear as you close your eyes and try to sleep at night.

percuss-- v. to verbally assault the percussion section.

percrastinate-- v. to wait until the last minute to fix precision problems in the percussion section.

perdiddle-- v. to vocalize percussion rudiments when explaining them (ex: "z-z-z-z-dot" = 9 stroke roll).

pseudoscaling-- v. the act of appearing confident while randomly moving fingers to an unfamiliar scale.

reedbed-- n. the little "mattresses" that reeds rest on in the box.

reed coffins-- n. individual plastic reed holders that reeds come in.

reedles-- n. small bits of cane which are scraped off a reed.

responesia-- n. a condition whereby a student energetically raises his hand to answer a question or make a comment and promptly forgets what he is going to say.

retroflap-- v. to conduct in wildly exaggerated motions when trying to get a musical group to slow down.

rohnergoo-- n. rubber-like substance which attaches various pull-out ads in *The Instrumentalist* and rips out half a page of the magazine when it finally breaks after stretching three feet.

sclission-- n. the pile-up which occurs when the first person in a follow-the-leader movement does a "to the rear" four counts early.

semi-drop--v. when a majorette drops a baton once during the halftime show (see also demisemidrop, hemidemisemidrop).

semitrash-- n. miscellaneous item which you don't feel you can throw away, but have absolutely no suitable place to store it.

shankmuck-- n. food particles left in a brass mouthpiece.

skank-- v. to dent a metal mute by using it to strike a glancing blow against a musical neighbor's knee.

slitters-- n. thin, leftover strips of paper which remain after using a paper-cutter on marching music.

snibble-- v. to scrape a reed.

smarch-- v. in marching, to take itty-bitty steps (when no one is looking) so that you are in line with everyone else.

smeartones-- n. in-between sounds on poorly played lip slurs.

sousaphobia-- n. the fear of Sousa marches.

spinal intonation adjustment-- n. the act of raising the neck and eyebrows to the highest position possible (with a slight tilt of the head forward) to indicate flatness of pitch to a student.

spivvle-- n. in brass playing, the airy, spitty sound which sometimes comes out on a high note instead of the intended tone.

splurping-- v. in woodwinds, the distasteful act of sucking in saliva from their mouthpieces.

stanwopped-- v. the process of raising a music stand and having the top fly off and hit you in the head.

standscum-- n. the black substance left on your fingers after fixing a music stand.

startrek-- v. in marching, to take a wrong turn and go where no marcher has gone before.

stringendoflap-- v. to wildly move arms and upper body in an effort to get the band to speed up the tempo.

subsquall-- n. sound produced when trying to play the lowest notes on a saxophone.

syncrostepping-- v. during marching season, unconsciously skip-stepping so that you are in step with others as you walk down the school hallway.

swablodge-- v. to lodge a clarinet swab in the top joint by pulling it in the wrong direction.

teedles-- n. small indentions on a timpani head.

telenesia-- n. the problem of dialing a phone number and forgetting whom you are calling just when the person answers.

tennistench-- n. odor of band lockers when tennis shoes worn during marching season have been in there for seven months.

Thompson syndrome-- n. the fear of tightening a Thompson mouthpiece puller too much and destroying a leadpipe.

upsy-daisyonics-- n. the habit directors have of raising their arms to conduct and after all the players raise their instruments, putting them down again to give one more tidbit of information.

worming-- v. in marching band, brass players who play with such a poor, downward horn position that only worms could hear the music.

yogle-- v. to produce any disgusting, nonmusical sound on a brass instrument, e.g., kissing sounds, etc.

ziljunk-- v. to incorrectly strike a pair of cymbals so that a dull thud is produced.

Index